The Ambitious Horse
Ancient Chin Mathematics Pro

Lawrence W. Swienciki, Ph.D.

Key Curriculum Press
Innovators in Mathematics Education

Project Editor: Anna Werner

Editorial Assistants: Beth Masse, Halo Golden

Reviewers: Dr. Robin D. S. Yates, McGill University, Montreal, Canada, and Tian Zaijin, Senior Editor, People's Education Press, Beijing, China

Consultant: Wei Zhang

Production Editor: Jennifer Strada

Copy Editor: Margaret Moore

Production and Manufacturing Manager: Diana Jean Parks

Production Coordinator: Laurel Roth Patton

Text Designer/Illustrator and Cover Illustrator: Lawrence W. Swienciki

Compositor: Kirk Mills

Art Editor: Jason Luz

Cover Designer: Caroline Ayres

Prepress and Printer: Malloy Lithographing, Inc.

Executive Editor: Casey FitzSimons

Publisher: Steven Rasmussen

Key Curriculum Press
1150 65th Street
Emeryville, CA 94608

510-595-7000

editorial@keypress.com

http://www.keypress.com

Printed in the United States of America

10 9 8 7 6 5 4 3 2   05 04   ISBN 1-55953-461-3

Contents

Algebra Integrated with Geometry

Preface

Over the last twenty years, there has been increased interest in using multicultural themes throughout the mathematics curriculum. This worthy goal is not an easy one for the mathematics classroom teacher because information of this type requires research. It is challenging to bring this information to students in a way that is meaningful to the mathematics curriculum.

In 1972, I began publishing multicultural math puzzles to reinforce basic skills in elementary algebra. My experience has been that materials of this kind bring various cultures to the classroom and provide an interesting way to reinforce math skills.

Multicultural material suitable for more advanced classes such as geometry, intermediate algebra, analysis, or calculus hasn't been widely available. As I pondered the idea of bringing a multicultural dimension into these courses, it was very clear to me that teaching time was at a premium. With students being taken out of class for field trips, class activities, counseling, and so on, I realized that it was impractical to introduce multicultural themes as a distinct lesson in advanced classes. It seemed to me that the most practical way to deal with the proposition that multicultural material could be incorporated into all math classes was to develop a series of posters recognizing mathematical achievements of various cultures. In this way teachers could have interesting materials to decorate their rooms, to accomplish multicultural content objectives, and to focus on their own curriculum, without getting into topics that would be difficult to connect to their objectives. As a consequence, I developed and published the *Math of Mexico* poster in 1980. Since then, many more international mathematics posters have been added to the series, recognizing the mathematical achievements of Africans, Chinese, Japanese, Indians, Native Americans, and others. Thus, at the present time, the poster series has not only met the original goal of providing multicultural references to all levels of math students, but has been an effective method of introducing the global history of mathematics.

Through my research in developing the poster series, it became apparent that more topics could be developed for teachers to use with the curriculum. The poster format did not provide the space needed to present all of these topics. My aim is to add resource books to the international mathematics poster series to provide more depth of information for teachers to use with their students.

I wish to take this opportunity to thank all of my benefactors who contributed to my education. In particular, I wish to thank the Sisters of the Presentation at St. Patrick's Elementary School in San Jose, California, and the Jesuit fathers at Bellarmine College Preparatory and Santa Clara University.

Lawrence W. Swienciki, Ph.D.

Santa Fe, New Mexico

June 29, 2000

Suggested Uses

When using multicultural material in a mathematics class, keep in mind your basic curriculum objectives. Multicultural themes can be a tool to motivate students, like the other tools you use to expand class activities such as math puzzles, math games, individual or group math projects, and student work at the chalkboard.

As teachers, we prepare students for the next mathematics class they take, while helping them to meet career challenges, and to appreciate the contributions of all cultures to our present-day knowledge. Multicultural content will enhance a mathematics class when it is presented in an interesting way for all students and especially when it reinforces the mathematics curriculum.

The Ambitious Horse: Ancient Chinese Mathematics Problems complements the international mathematics poster *Math of China* offered by Key Curriculum Press. This book focuses on ancient and medieval Chinese mathematics. There is a broad range of topics in this book that can serve a variety of needs for teachers and students. There are sections that deal with elementary level, secondary level, and college level mathematics. Topics in this book were chosen to make it possible for teachers and students to use Chinese mathematics that can be connected to modern curriculum. In fact, this volume is designed to be reproducible for instructional purposes.

Elementary and Middle School Level

At the elementary and middle school level, teachers can find topics on the base-10 number system, operations on the Chinese calculating board. For example, "Calculator Rod Addition" is a manipulative activity—very much like a game—that can increase understanding of place value. Also, the seven-piece puzzle is another manipulative activity that promotes basic skills in geometry. A teacher at the elementary school level will find the presentation in this book well-suited for the elementary school environment where curriculum is generally more integrated than secondary or college level curriculum. Topics presented in this book integrate mathematics, history, art, and culture.

High School Level

Several topics relate directly to the subjects of elementary algebra, geometry, and intermediate algebra. Teachers can find applications with traditional lessons or activities in such classes. Moreover, students have opportunities to solve problems with alternate methodologies. For example, the problem "The Ambitious Horse" provides a Chinese solution that is different from most Western explanations of problems on arithmetic series. That students can view multiple methods of solving a given problem is valuable in developing critical thinking—this experience encourages them to be more reflective.

College Level

There are problems involving the solution of polynomial equations of arbitrary degree from the area of algebra known as the theory of equations. Problems are developed in number theory related to operations with modular arithmetic. These and other topics can be especially valuable in a history of mathematics class or for students preparing to become teachers.

Mathematics Projects

Some topics in this book can be used for individual or group activity projects—in particular, the topics on extracting roots or solving polynomial equations. Another project taking the students outdoors involves the ancient Chinese mathematics of surveying.

Home School or Specialized Schools

Home schooling has become more popular in recent years. With this resource book, parents can provide their children a broad range of historical mathematics that is fundamentally sound. The material in this book offers opportunities for projects or activities.

Some Chinese-American students attend special classes on Chinese culture because they or their parents value the opportunity to learn about their cultural heritage. This book can be used by teachers offering such classes or by students studying at home, self-directed or assisted by parents or family.

Below.

The Great Wall of China is the most spectacular wall ever built. The central part stretches 1,500 miles across northern China from the Yellow Sea to the central Asian desert. This symbol of China was built by General Meng Tian on orders from the first emperor of China, Qin Shihuangdi, who unified China in 221 B.C. General Meng linked earlier walls together to make the Great Wall.

Chinese Writing

"Jing xi zi zhi"

The inventions of paper (second to first centuries B.C.), printing with wooden blocks (eighth century), and movable type (eleventh century) are accolades to China's writing tradition. This tradition, the longest and most continuous of any nation, defines Chinese culture more than any other characteristic.

Two anecdotes demonstrate how important the writing tradition is to the Chinese people. First, in ancient China to carelessly throw paper with writing into the street was considered disrespectful to the written word. Second, as late as the 1930s in Beijing, public trash containers bore the phrase *Jing xi zi zhi*—"Respect and save written paper."

Scientists have discovered Neolithic cultures in China dating before 6000 B.C., but the earliest written history begins with the late Shang dynasty (approximately 1250 to 1050 B.C.) with inscriptions on oracle bones and cast bronze artifacts.

The writing tradition of China is very different from that of other cultures, and it has enjoyed a unity and continuity for thousands of years. Chinese graphs are composed of two parts: a signific or radical, indicating the general category to which the word belongs; and a phonetic, which gives its approximate sound. Only a small portion of these complex graphs were originally actual pictures, such as a horse or a flag.

In spite of the stability of Chinese writing, China's long history before unification in 221 B.C. was subject to intense wars that destroyed the written records of the defeated. Therefore much early evidence for the history of writing has been lost. Fortunately, new archaeological discoveries have provided historians and scientists with fresh material for understanding the history of the formation of numerals. Some discoveries even suggest that basic Chinese numerals appear scratched on pottery dating from 5000 B.C.

The concept of counting is elementary in any culture. Scientists have not provided a complete history of the development of numerals in China, but it is ancient and parallels the development of writing over thousands of years. There is also evidence that growth of the numeral system was subject to change and variations. For example, coins cast during the second century B.C. and used for hundreds of years bear numerals that are now discontinued in Chinese writing.

On the *Math of China* poster, the numerals displayed in the 40 boxes of the poster represent the traditional or literary method of writing Chinese numerals. However, four major types of numerals have developed in China: a traditional or literary form, a business or legal form, a calculating rod form, and an abbreviated form. The symbols in the center of the *Math of China* poster, the *Ba Gua,* are not numerals but, rather, mathematical permutations of the symbols for the Chinese concepts of *yin* and *yang.*

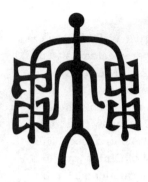

Above.

Shang dynasty characters were inscribed on divination bones and cast bronze artifacts as early as 1250–1050 B.C.

**yi
er
san
si
wu
liu
qi
ba
jiu
shi
bai
qian
wan**

Above.

The romanized names for
the Chinese numerals: (top
to bottom) 1 through 10,
100, 1,000, and 10,000.

Traditional Numerals

Chinese numerals, just as our own
Hindu-Arabic symbols, are based on
powers of 10. Although they can be written
from left to right, the traditional form is
to write them vertically from top to bottom.
Some of the most commonly used numerals
are illustrated in the student instruction
charts on pages 5 and 6.

To write other numerals, such as multiples of
10, the symbols from 1 to 10 are employed
with the idea of place value. For example,
think of 60 as 6 × 10. In the Chinese system,
put the character for 6 over the character for
10 to represent 60 as shown below.

To write the numeral for 600, think of 600 as
6 × 100. Similar to the previous example,
write the 6 over the 100 symbol in the
Chinese system as shown below.

Numerals such as 6,000 follow the same
pattern. Think of 6,000 as 6 × 1,000. For
Chinese numerals, write 6 over 1,000 as
illustrated below.

At right.

The three examples
illustrate the property of
place value. The Chinese
use a special character
for place value. Modern
Hindu-Arabic notation
uses position to show
place value.

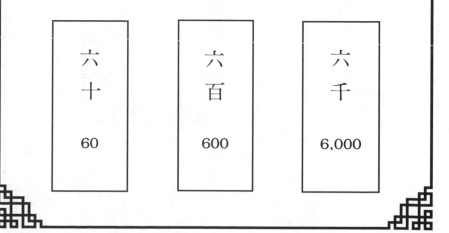

六 十	六 百	六 千
60	600	6,000

To write numerals such as 250, think of 250 as $(2 \times 100) + (5 \times 10)$. In the Chinese system, start at the top with 2 over the 100. Continue under the 100 with the 5 over the 10. This is shown at the bottom of the page.

To write four-digit numerals such as 1,492, think of 1,492 as $(1 \times 1,000) + (4 \times 100) + (9 \times 10) + 2$. The Chinese representation follows the same pattern as the last example and is illustrated below.

Ling Symbol for Zero

If 1,066 is written as the sum of powers of 10, then $1,066 = (1 \times 1,000) + (0 \times 100) + (6 \times 10) + 6$. However, the Chinese did not always have a zero in their system of mathematics. Think of 1,066 as $(1 \times 1,000) + (6 \times 10) + 6$. To help the reader quickly understand that a multiple of 10 follows the 1,000, the symbol 零 is placed between the 1,000 and the 6 symbol as illustrated below.

Above.

During the Ming dynasty (1368–1644), the Chinese character *ling* was adopted as zero in writing numerals in both traditional and accountant forms. The ancient meaning of *ling* is the small droplet of water left on a plant or some object after a rainstorm. It is speculated that the name was applied to the Sanskrit O introduced in the previous dynasty, the Song (960–1279).

At left.

The three examples illustrate more complex Chinese numerals. The example for 1,066 has a symbol that acts as a zero but is not a numeral. It can be understood as a Chinese punctuation symbol. The numeral O came from India. However, it was not introduced into Chinese mathematics until the middle of the thirteenth century A.D.

250

1,492

1,066

Instruction Chart

Below are characters commonly used in writing Chinese numerals. You can use this chart as a reference to form the more complex examples found in some of the exercises.

一 1	二 2	三 3	四 4
五 5	六 6	七 7	八 8
九 9	十 10	百 100	千 1,000
十一 11	十二 12	十三 13	十四 14

Below.

Dragon design from the Tang dynasty (618–907 A.D.)

More Complex Examples

The characters in the diagram below represent symbols that are more complex than those found on page 5. You can use this chart to analyze the construction of Chinese numerals. It can also help you complete the exercises that follow.

十五	十六	十七	十八
15	16	17	18
二十	三十	四十	五十
20	30	40	50
一百二十五	四百九十八	七百六十	八百
125	498	760	800
一百零一	一千七百四十	一千八百六十	一千九百四十五
101	1,740	1,860	1,945

Exercise 1

Use the charts on pages 5 and 6 as a guide in writing the modern Hindu-Arabic equivalents to the Chinese numerals below. For each window, write the answer in the box below the Chinese characters.

四	八	六	九

十三	十	百	七

十四	五十	三百六十五	九百九十九

一百零一	二千七百七十六	六百八十七	一千九百八十二

Below.

Ancient Chinese graph for long life (*shou*).

Exercise 2

In each window below, there is either a Chinese or Hindu-Arabic numeral. Convert each numeral to the other writing system. Fill in the empty spaces above or below the given characters.

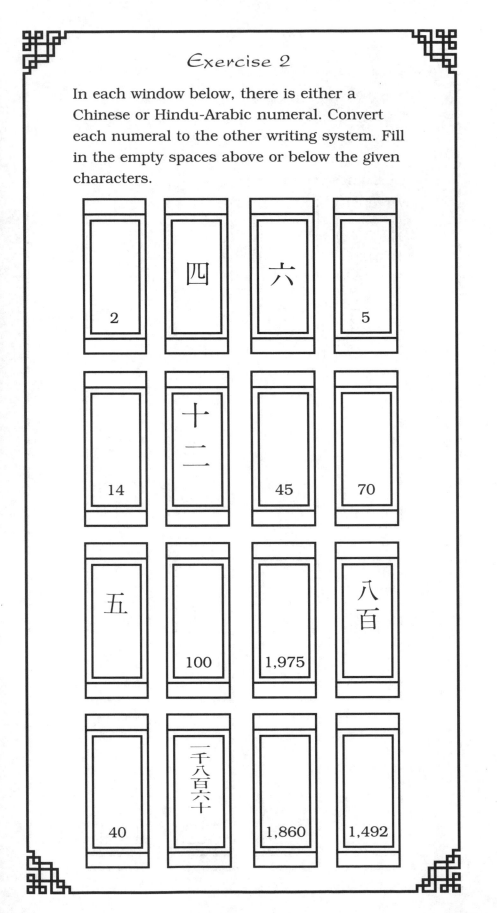

Below.

Ancient Chinese graph for joy (*le*).

Exercise 3

The example below demonstrates the property of place value. The Chinese numeral inside the window is written as a sum of powers of 10 and as a single numeral in modern Hindu-Arabic notation. Complete Exercises a–f found below and on page 10.

Example

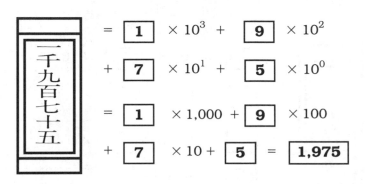

二千九百七十五

$$= \boxed{1} \times 10^3 + \boxed{9} \times 10^2$$
$$+ \boxed{7} \times 10^1 + \boxed{5} \times 10^0$$
$$= \boxed{1} \times 1{,}000 + \boxed{9} \times 100$$
$$+ \boxed{7} \times 10 + \boxed{5} = \boxed{1{,}975}$$

a.

二千九百八十二

$$= \boxed{} \times 10^3 + \boxed{} \times 10^2$$
$$+ \boxed{} \times 10^1 + \boxed{} \times 10^0$$
$$= \boxed{} \times 1{,}000 + \boxed{} \times 100$$
$$+ \boxed{} \times 10 + \boxed{} = \boxed{}$$

b.

二千七百四十

$$= \boxed{} \times 10^3 + \boxed{} \times 10^2$$
$$+ \boxed{} \times 10^1 + \boxed{} \times 10^0$$
$$= \boxed{} \times 1{,}000 + \boxed{} \times 100$$
$$+ \boxed{} \times 10 + \boxed{} = \boxed{}$$

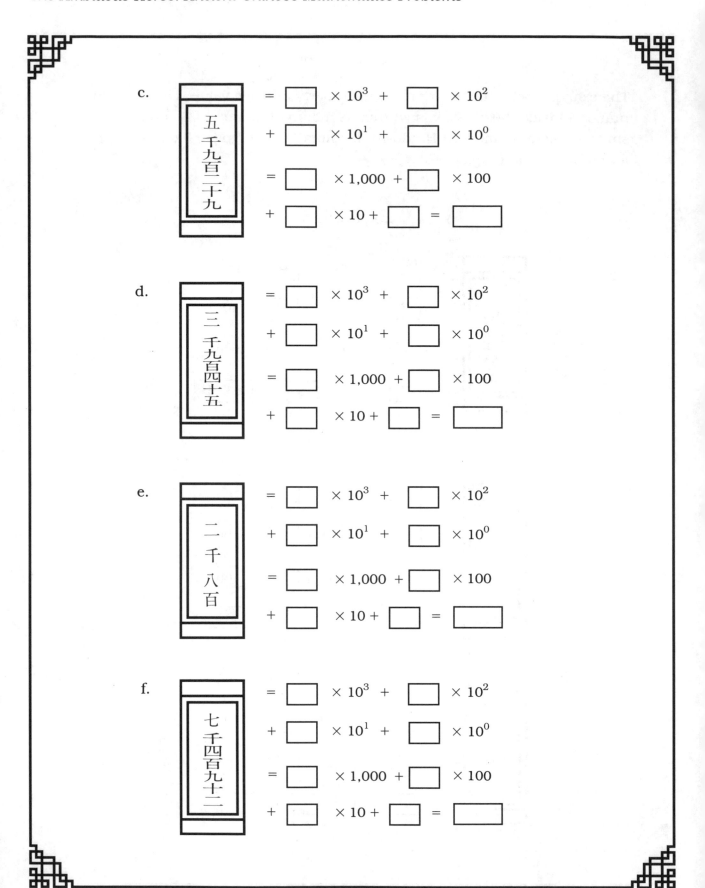

c. 五千九百二十九

$= \boxed{} \times 10^3 + \boxed{} \times 10^2$

$+ \boxed{} \times 10^1 + \boxed{} \times 10^0$

$= \boxed{} \times 1{,}000 + \boxed{} \times 100$

$+ \boxed{} \times 10 + \boxed{} = \boxed{}$

d. 三千九百四十五

$= \boxed{} \times 10^3 + \boxed{} \times 10^2$

$+ \boxed{} \times 10^1 + \boxed{} \times 10^0$

$= \boxed{} \times 1{,}000 + \boxed{} \times 100$

$+ \boxed{} \times 10 + \boxed{} = \boxed{}$

e. 二千八百

$= \boxed{} \times 10^3 + \boxed{} \times 10^2$

$+ \boxed{} \times 10^1 + \boxed{} \times 10^0$

$= \boxed{} \times 1{,}000 + \boxed{} \times 100$

$+ \boxed{} \times 10 + \boxed{} = \boxed{}$

f. 七千四百九十二

$= \boxed{} \times 10^3 + \boxed{} \times 10^2$

$+ \boxed{} \times 10^1 + \boxed{} \times 10^0$

$= \boxed{} \times 1{,}000 + \boxed{} \times 100$

$+ \boxed{} \times 10 + \boxed{} = \boxed{}$

Exercise 4

Complete the multiplication grid below. Multiply the corresponding numbers and write the answers in the spaces provided. The rectangular spaces will allow you to write Chinese characters vertically.

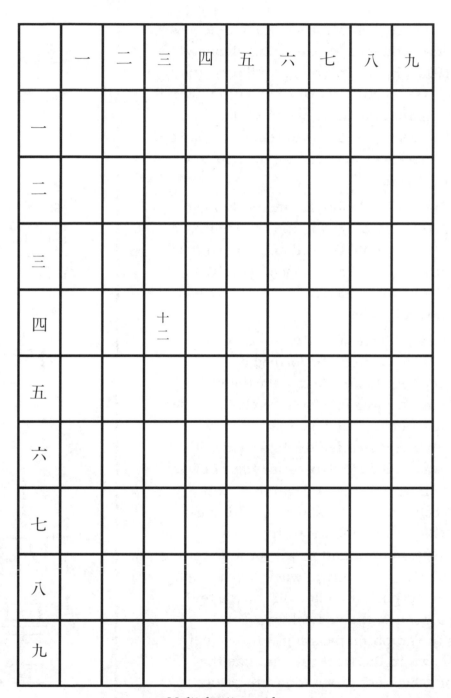

	一	二	三	四	五	六	七	八	九
一									
二									
三									
四			十二						
五									
六									
七									
八									
九									

Multiplication grid

The Emperor's Last Will

In 1662 the great emperor Kangxi ascended the throne of the Manchu, or Qing, dynasty (1644–1911). His reign brought military unity to China. He greatly favored the continuation of learning from the Ming dynasty. However, he allowed corrupt officials to remain in office and was indecisive in declaring his heir to the throne of China.

Legend has it that before his death, Kangxi designated his favorite son, the fourteenth, to be his heir. He wrote the will and named his fourteenth son to take his place upon his death. The will was hidden in a secret spot behind a royal tablet.

The emperor's secret was discovered by his fourth son, Yongzheng. He formed a conspiracy with his uncle to alter the will. A kung-fu master was employed to climb to the hidden location and change the will to read the fourth son instead of the fourteenth. This change was easily made because the will was not written with formal or legal numerals. The left column at right shows what Kangxi wrote: "Give reign to fourteenth prince." Notice the traditional numerals for fourteen are used. The ten numeral was easily altered by drawing a horizontal line on the top and adding a hook to the vertical line. This creates the graph *yu* meaning "to." The new form, shown in the right column, has the meaning "Give the throne to fourth prince."

Below.

Left column designates the fourteenth son as heir to the throne of China in traditional literary form of numerals. Right column names the fourth son in the same way.

傳位十四皇子 傳位于四皇子

Chinese Legal Numerals

When Kangxi died, Yongzheng the fourth son became emperor. Thus, China's history had been changed by the misuse of writing simple numeral characters.

If Kangxi had been careful in making his will, he would have used formal, or accountant, numerals. For legal documents, China had centuries before developed special characters to prevent such fraud. Shown in the caption at left is the legal method the emperor could have chosen. The left column designates the fourteenth prince as heir, while the right column designates the fourth prince.

At the bottom of the page, two examples of writing numerals are given in both traditional and accountant form. Compare these numerals to the example of 101 on page 6. Notice the *ling* zero symbol is used only once in 1,001. This is another indication that the symbol is not a true mathematical zero, but a punctuation symbol indicating that place value is being skipped between numerals.

Below.

Left column designates the fourteenth son as heir to the throne of China using formal, or accountant, numerals. Right column names the fourth son in the same manner.

傳　傳
位　位
位　于
拾　肆
肆　皇
皇　子
子

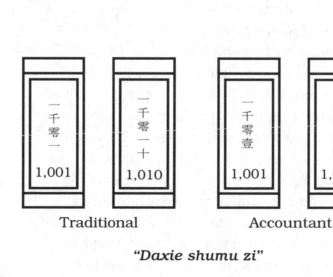

一千零一	一千零一十	一千零壹	一千零壹拾
1,001	1,010	1,001	1,010
Traditional		Accountant	

"Daxie shumu zi"

The Calculating Rods of Ancient China

For at least 2,000 years, Chinese mathematicians used an amazing system of calculating rods to solve a wide range of problems. Originally the rods were large, but a variety of types developed over the centuries. A classic set might consist of 271 small bamboo pieces about 4 cm long and 0.5 cm in diameter. Red pieces represented positive numbers, and black ones stood for negative numbers. The illustration depicts their use on a rectangular grid called a *counting board*.

Calculating rod numerals are based on the decimal system with a set of nine digits. Oracle bone inscriptions suggest that the Shang Chinese were the first known people to possess such a system in the ancient world. The nine digits are defined in Figure 1 on page 15. Mathematicians used two forms: one for odd powers of 10, another for even powers of 10. This system served as a check against error and made the numerals easier to read. Unlike the literary form for Chinese numerals, there are no special symbols for place value for calculating rod numerals. The rod numerals use position for place value and are read from left to right.

Chinese Rod Numerals

Ones, Hundreds, Ten Thousands

Tens, Thousands, Hundred Thousands

FIGURE 1

Two examples of writing rod numerals are shown in Figure 2. Notice the sevens in the rod numerals for 1,776 are written in two ways because one of the numerals is a multiple of 100 and the other is a multiple of 10.

1,776   365

FIGURE 2

The numerals in Figure 2 are not customarily written on paper. Instead, they are rods of bamboo, ivory, iron, or wood placed on a grid called a *counting board.* The far right column of the grid represents the *ones* place value. The column to the left of the ones is the *tens.* The pattern of place value for other columns proceeds in the same form as does the modern decimal system for whole numbers.

The numerals in Figure 2 posed no problem in writing on paper with rod numeral symbols, but when writing numerals such as 3,605 or 17,760 we do not know how to deal with the zero. On the counting board, there is no difficulty because a blank square is left for the zero. It wasn't until the eighth century A.D. that the O symbol from India was introduced into China. Ever since the Ming dynasty (1368–1644), the O has been utilized when writing out rod numerals on paper. In Figure 3, rod numerals for 3,605 and 17,760 are shown as they appeared in documents after the late Ming period.

17,760   3,605

FIGURE 3

Rod numerals are designed to be used for mathematics in the same way that the abacus or modern calculator is used to speed computation. Calculating rods are placed on a counting board from left to right. Operations such as addition, subtraction, multiplication, division, and finding square roots or even higher roots are made easier. Ancient Chinese mathematicians were able to solve many advanced algebraic problems with this tool.

The Chinese through the fourteenth century were ahead of most other peoples in mathematics. At that time no country had developed a convenient symbolic notation. Instead, problems were usually written out in words. The counting board with the rod numerals made it possible to solve advanced problems without the use of symbolic notation. However, in time this feature became a limitation to Chinese mathematics. China needed a symbolic notation to carry it beyond the glorious achievements of its past.

Rod Numeral Operations

Rod numeral operations on the counting board often involved more than one person. Numbers were called out by one individual, and a second person placed or moved the calculating pieces on the board. Because the number of operations left on the board at any one time was limited to the size of the board, steps were generally replaced through the solution of the problem. In our explanation of the calculating rods, the ordinary use of this device has a different style than it does on paper. It is suggested that you make a simple grid on paper. Using flat toothpicks for rod numerals, manipulate the pieces on the board for the various problems. In this way you sense the power of this calculating tool.

Calculating Rod Addition

The examples shown in Figures 1 and 2 on page 18 demonstrate the operation of addition with the calculating rods. The first example, 345 + 271, shows the result, 616, on the third row of the counting board. The rod numerals are aligned in the same manner as in modern arithmetic.

In the second example, 4,809 + 718 = 5,527. The 4,809 has a zero in the tens place. On the counting board, Figure 2 illustrates the rod numerals for 4,809 on the first line with a blank space where the zero occurs. Otherwise, the second example follows the same pattern as the first. Try this process with a column of numbers to be summed. But, instead of filling up the rows with symbols, ask someone to call out the numbers to you. In this way you will sense the speed of not writing down all the numerals. You can change the partial sums as the process continues in the same way it was done in ancient China.

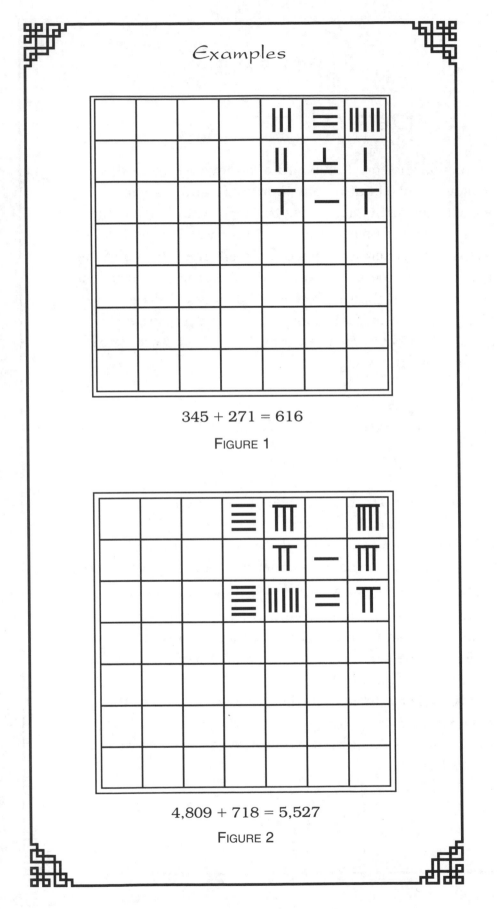

Examples

345 + 271 = 616

FIGURE 1

4,809 + 718 = 5,527

FIGURE 2

Below.

Tang dynasty symbol for long life.

Above.

The Song dynasty (960–1279) introduced monograms formed of rod numerals useful for table entries. The rod numeral for 4,716 is shown in monogram form.

Calculating Rod Subtraction

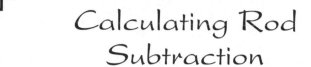

The example of subtraction comes from the Song dynasty. The mathematician Qin Jiushao wrote the subtraction problem 1,470,000 − 64,464 = 1,405,536 in his book *Shushu jiuzhang* (*Computational Techniques in Nine Chapters*), published in 1247, as shown at the bottom of the page.

In Figure 3 on page 20, the same problem is represented on the counting board with the rod numerals. Notice in Qin Jiushao's writing of the results on paper, the *ling* symbol O was used. Furthermore, the book illustrates the fact that at various times and locations in China, some mathematicians used varied forms of rod numerals such as the crossed rods for the numeral 4. Try the problem on the counting board yourself. The problem requires you to borrow. What is the simplest method of borrowing using the rod numerals?

In Figure 4 on page 20, another example of a subtraction problem is displayed on a counting board for you to verify. In Figures 5 and 6, the subtraction problems are displayed on the counting board, but you will have to fill in the boxes below the boards in modern Hindu-Arabic notation.

ΙΞΟΞΙΙΙΙΞΤ   ΙΞΠΟΟΟΟ
                            Τ × ΙΙΙΙ ⊥ ×

Examples

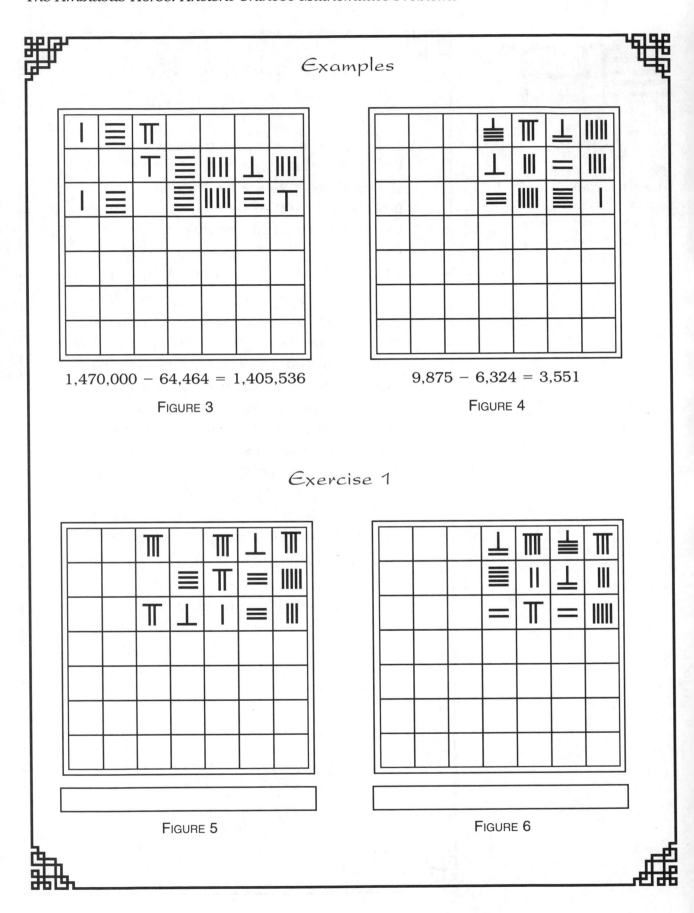

$1,470,000 - 64,464 = 1,405,536$

FIGURE 3

$9,875 - 6,324 = 3,551$

FIGURE 4

Exercise 1

FIGURE 5

FIGURE 6

Exercise 2

The problems below provide you with practice recognizing the rod numerals. Use Figure 1 on page 15 as a guide to complete the boxes. If the rod numerals are represented on a single row of the counting board, write the modern Hindu-Arabic numerals in the box to the right of the problem. For the Hindu-Arabic numerals given in the box, fill in the counting board row with rod numerals.

a. | | | ≡ | T | ⊥ | ╥ | =   [   ]

b. | ╓ | ⊥ | ╥ | ≝ | |||| | =   [   ]

c. [| | | | | | |]   =   [1,249   ]

d. [| | | | | | | |]   =   [8,203   ]

e. [| | | ≡ | | ⊥ | T]   =   [   ]

f. [| | | | | | | |]   =   [8,772   ]

g. [| | | | | | |]   =   [42,365   ]

h. | ╓ | ⊥ | T | ≡ | || | =   [   ]

i. [| | | | | | |]   =   [294,786   ]

j. | ╥ | | ╓ | ≡ | ╓ | ≝ | =   [   ]

Exercise 3

Complete the following addition or subtraction problems with rod numerals. Each problem is written in modern Hindu-Arabic numerals below the counting board. Fill in the appropriate squares with rod numeral symbols, and complete the problem by adding or subtracting on the board. Verify your answers with ordinary arithmetic.

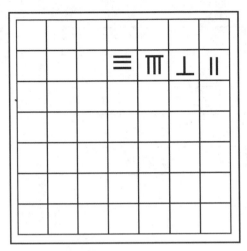

a.   798,325 + 3,862

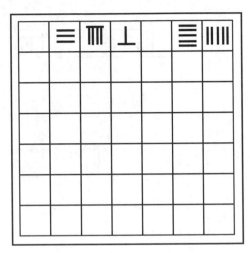

b.   396,055 + 10,309

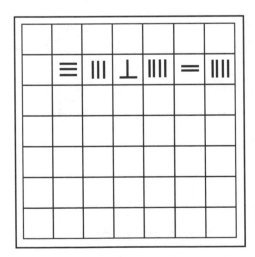

c.   897,538 − 336,424

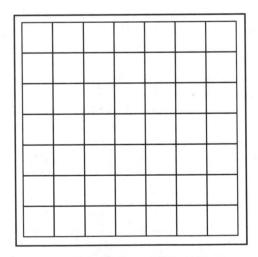

d.   472,935 − 129,476

Exercise 4

In this exercise, rod numeral problems involving addition or subtraction are displayed on calculating-board grids. Convert each problem into modern Hindu-Arabic notation by filling in the box below the grid with appropriate numerals and operation symbols.

a.

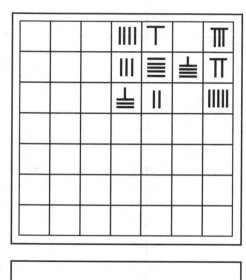

b.

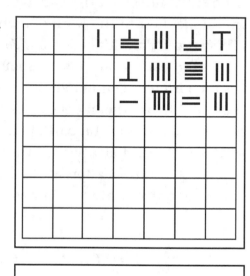

c.

d.

The Chariot Driver

Ancient Chinese mathematicians compared multiplication to the work of a chariot driver. The word for multiplication, *chêng,* had the general meaning "to ride on something," such as a charioteer commanding a team of horses. The mathematician was considered to be in control of the partial sums in the process of multiplication. In this way of thinking, multiplication was a shortcut for carrying out repeated additions.

Ancient Chinese Multiplication

Two examples of multiplication with calculating rods are shown with the use of detailed diagrams over the next few pages. However, you can understand the process better by making a square grid and using flat toothpicks for calculating rods. Although there is no standard size grid, use a grid with seven rows and seven columns for the examples.

上位
SHANG WEI

中位
ZHONG WEI

下位
XIA WEI

Above.

The three basic terms in Chinese multiplication are *shang wei,* multiplier; *zhong wei,* product; *xia wei,* multiplicand. These three terms appear on Chinese mathematical commentaries but are not written on the counting board.

Example 1

The sequence of three board patterns on page 26 illustrates the multiplication of 49 × 25. The first caption of the problem contains the commentary marks for the operations. The multiplier, 49, is placed at the top right on the board. At the very bottom of the board, the multiplicand, 25, is placed. Note that its last digit, 5, aligns with the first digit, 4, in the multiplier. This alignment is the usual way of starting the problem. The partial products and partial sums are done between the top and bottom rows.

In the second caption, the 4 in the multiplier and the entire multiplicand are more heavily framed for emphasis in the explanation. The 4 in the multiplier is applied to the 25 of the multiplicand. The first product, 4 × 2 = 8, is obtained. The 8 is written in the second row directly above the 2 because the place value position on the board makes the product really 40 × 20 = 800. In the diagram this is annotated at the left of the second row. In daily practice it is not necessary to think of the actual place value. The product is always written above the digit in the multiplicand. If the product has two digits, an additional column space to the left is used.

Next, multiply the 4 in the multiplier and the 5 in the multiplicand: 4 × 5 = 20, two digits. The zero, which is not marked on the board, aligns with the 5 in row three. The 2 must be written to the left of the zero position. The side note in the figure justifies this process since 40 × 5 = 200.

In the last caption, the pieces are moved to show the first partial sum in row two. The multiplicand is moved to the right one space. Notice that the multiplicand does not change symbols when its column position is moved. No notation change occurs because the operations are performed between the first and last rows.

In the last caption, the 9 in the multiplier is heavily framed with the multiplicand to indicate which numbers are used next. 9 × 2 = 18. Write 18 in row three above the 2 digit of the multiplicand. But 18 has two digits. Therefore, enter 8 above the 2 and 1 to the left. Next multiply 9 times 5. Enter 45 in row four. Add rows two, three, and four to obtain the final sum, 1,225.

Problem: 49 × 25

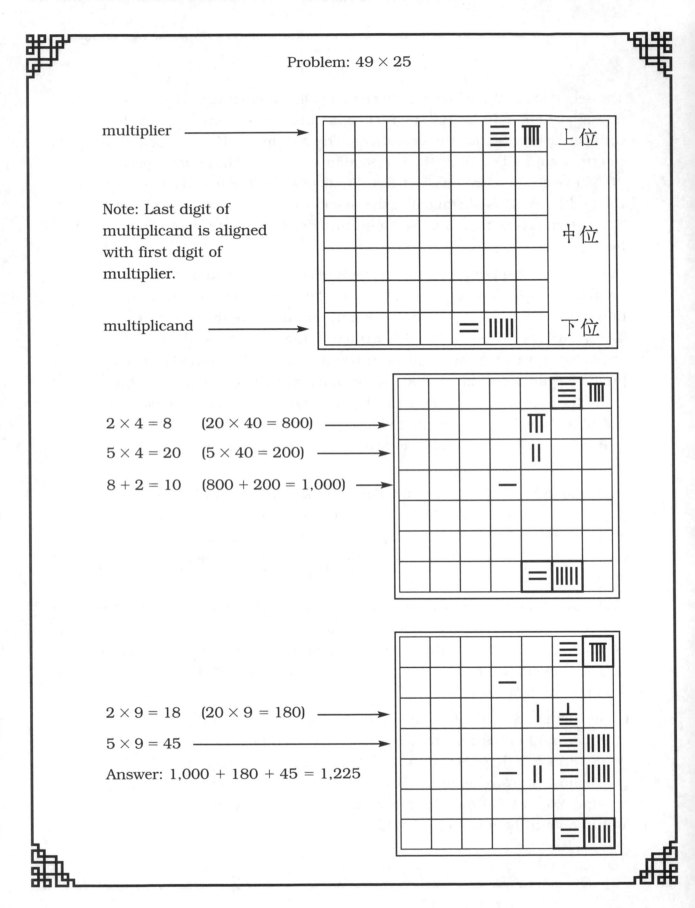

multiplier

Note: Last digit of multiplicand is aligned with first digit of multiplier.

multiplicand

2 × 4 = 8   (20 × 40 = 800)
5 × 4 = 20   (5 × 40 = 200)
8 + 2 = 10   (800 + 200 = 1,000)

2 × 9 = 18   (20 × 9 = 180)
5 × 9 = 45
Answer: 1,000 + 180 + 45 = 1,225

Example 2

The second example of multiplication with calculating rods is 736×298. The process is shown in four captions beginning at the bottom of this page. The pattern is similar to the first example but involves larger numbers. The explanation is condensed.

The caption below shows the given problem with the multiplier at the top and the multiplicand at the bottom. Note the alignment of first and last digits.

In the second caption, at the top of page 28, the 7 is multiplied over the multiplicand. The three partial products are entered in rows two, three, and four. The three rows are added. The partial sum is entered in row five.

In the third caption, the multiplicand is shifted to the right one space. The pieces are moved, with the partial sum from the previous diagram entered in row two. Next, 3 in the multiplier operates on the multiplicand. The three partial products are entered and summed. Row five is the second partial sum. The latter sum is carried to row two of the last caption on page 28.

In the fourth caption, the multiplicand is moved one last time to the right. The 6 in the multiplier operates on the multiplicand. The three partial products are entered and summed to get the final answer in line five.

Problem: 736×298

multiplier ⟶

Note: Last digit of multiplicand is aligned with first digit of multiplier.

multiplicand ⟶

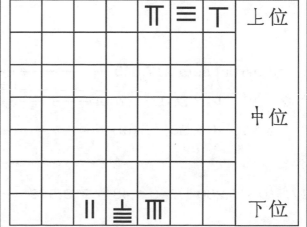

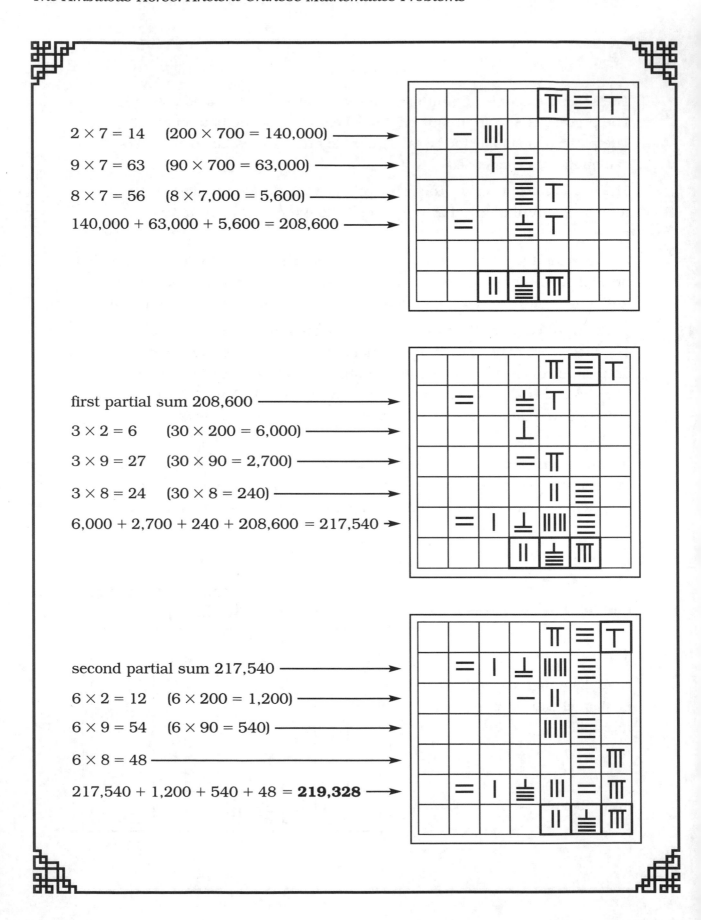

$2 \times 7 = 14$ $(200 \times 700 = 140{,}000)$ ⟶

$9 \times 7 = 63$ $(90 \times 700 = 63{,}000)$ ⟶

$8 \times 7 = 56$ $(8 \times 7{,}000 = 5{,}600)$ ⟶

$140{,}000 + 63{,}000 + 5{,}600 = 208{,}600$ ⟶

first partial sum 208,600 ⟶

$3 \times 2 = 6$ $(30 \times 200 = 6{,}000)$ ⟶

$3 \times 9 = 27$ $(30 \times 90 = 2{,}700)$ ⟶

$3 \times 8 = 24$ $(30 \times 8 = 240)$ ⟶

$6{,}000 + 2{,}700 + 240 + 208{,}600 = 217{,}540$ ⟶

second partial sum 217,540 ⟶

$6 \times 2 = 12$ $(6 \times 200 = 1{,}200)$ ⟶

$6 \times 9 = 54$ $(6 \times 90 = 540)$ ⟶

$6 \times 8 = 48$ ⟶

$217{,}540 + 1{,}200 + 540 + 48 = \textbf{219{,}328}$ ⟶

Exercise 1

Each counting board below has a multiplication to be performed. Write down in modern numerical symbols what the problem is. Then use the calculating rods on a counting board to perform the multiplication. Check your answer by ordinary multiplication or with a calculator.

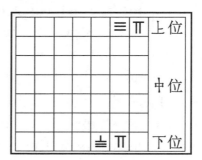

a. The product the board is set for you to solve is _____ .

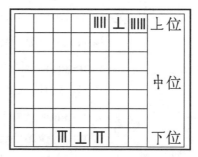

b. The product the board is set for you to solve is _____ .

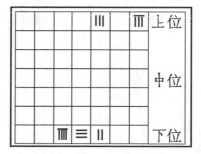

c. The product the board is set for you to solve is _____ .

Below.

Confucius or Kong Qiu (551–479 B.C.) was China's most influential teacher. He trained his students in the "Six Arts," one of which was mathematics. He considered his work a failure because he could not reform the politics of his time. But his teaching through the work of his students has had a monumental effect on Chinese life for many centuries.

Seven-Piece Puzzle

The Seven-Piece Puzzle is an ancient Chinese amusement that has remained popular through the centuries. The puzzle, traditionally made of wood, consists of seven wooden polygons neatly fitted together to form a square. The figure at right illustrates what the pieces are.

The object of the puzzle is to rearrange the pieces in different shapes. You can make a model and experiment with the pieces to see what shapes you can make. The dimensions of the pieces are provided below. The numbers correspond to the pieces in the figure for future reference.

Piece 1:	square with unit side
Pieces 2 and 3:	isosceles right triangle with unit legs
Piece 4:	isosceles right triangle with hypotenuse of 2 units
Piece 5:	parallelogram with unit base and unit height
Pieces 6 and 7:	isosceles right triangle with legs of 2 units

七巧板

Above.

Ancient Chinese characters representing the classic Seven-Piece Puzzle.

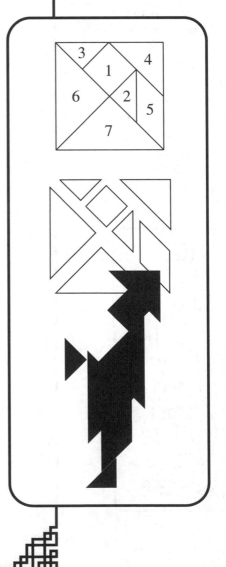

Below.

Shou, symbol for longevity, from a nineteenth-century silk robe of a mandarin.

Exercises: Seven-Piece Puzzle

1. In the figure shown on page 30, the pieces are separated and rearranged to form the shaded figure of a person with a fan. Use the model you constructed to create this figure.

2. What is the area of the figure you constructed in the first question above? Express your answer in square units.

3. Arrange the Seven-Piece Puzzle to form the shaded figures of a kangaroo and a crane shown below. What is the area of the kangaroo figure in square units? What is the area of the crane figure in square units?

4. Write a statement about the area of the three figures you constructed from the Seven-Piece Puzzle. Write a hypothesis for a general case.

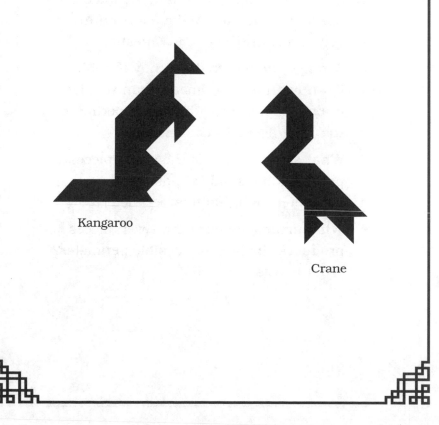

Kangaroo

Crane

Exercise with the Dog

1. Arrange the Seven-Piece Puzzle to make the figure of the dog shown at right. What is the area of the figure in square units?

2. Form any pattern you like with the Seven-Piece Puzzle, but make the pattern a single closed region.

3. Estimate the distance around the figure. Define this as the perimeter.

4. Can you increase or decrease the perimeter by sliding the pieces along their common edges while still maintaining a single closed region?

5. From Question 4, estimate the minimum possible perimeter. Make a sketch of the original figure and the new one with the minimum perimeter.

6. From Question 4, estimate the maximum possible perimeter. Make a sketch to compare with the one in Question 4.

7. Arrange the pieces differently to make a figure with less perimeter than the figure in Question 5, or with greater perimeter than the figure in Question 6.

8. What arrangement of the seven pieces produces the smallest possible perimeter? What is this perimeter?

9. What arrangement of the seven pieces produces the largest possible perimeter? What is this perimeter?

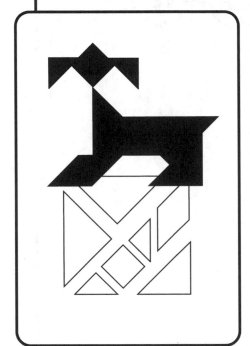

Chinese Dissections

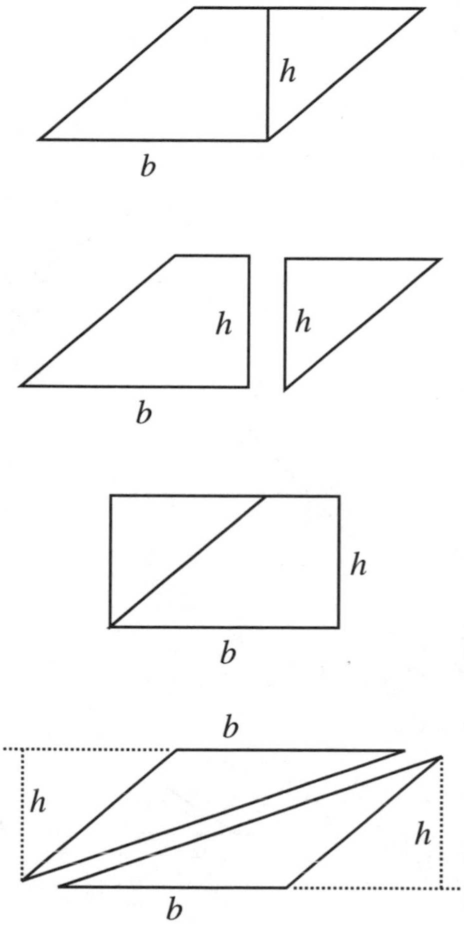

Dissection can be used to discover formulas for the areas of geometric figures such as parallelograms, triangles, trapezoids, and other polygons. For example, starting with the formula for the area of a rectangle as the product of its base and altitude, the formula for the area of a parallelogram follows easily by dissection.

At the left a parallelogram is depicted. To find a formula for its area, A_p, dissect the parallelogram along the segment representing its altitude to obtain a trapezoid and a right triangle. Can you state what the area of a parallelogram is? Use the diagrams at left to prove your formula.

From the parallelogram the area formula for a triangle easily follows. Dissect the parallelogram along one of its diagonals. Use the formula that you derived and refer to the diagram at left to prove that the area of a triangle is

$$A_t = \frac{1}{2}bh$$

Classic Theorem

One of the fundamental theorems of Euclidean geometry is that the sum of the interior angles of any triangle is 180 degrees. A simple proof can be made using dissection.

In the figure to the right, a triangle is given. You will prove that $\angle A + \angle B + \angle C = 180°$. Draw any triangle ABC and proceed with the following construction.

1. Construct segment MN so that M and N are midpoints of segments AC and BC, respectively.

2. Construct segments MX and NY perpendicular to segment AB.

3. Label for simplicity the three interior angles as shown in the second figure as $\angle 1$, $\angle 2$, $\angle 3$.

4. By dissection, $\triangle AMX$, $\triangle MCN$, and $\triangle BYN$ can be separated and reflected over MX, MN, and NY, respectively, to form the rectangle $MNYX$ in the third figure.

   From the last figure: Prove that $\angle 1$, $\angle 2$, and $\angle 3$ form a straight angle. In other words, the reflected images of points A, B, and C are the same and on AB. Therefore, $\angle 1 + \angle 2 + \angle 3 = 180°$. Why? Finally, $\angle A + \angle B + \angle C = 180°$. Why?

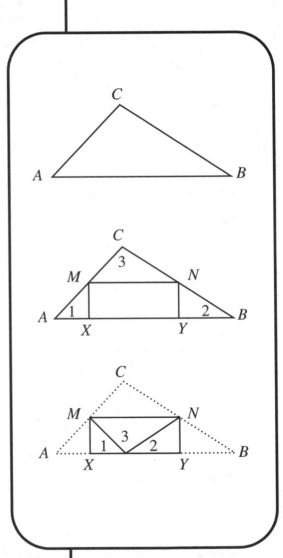

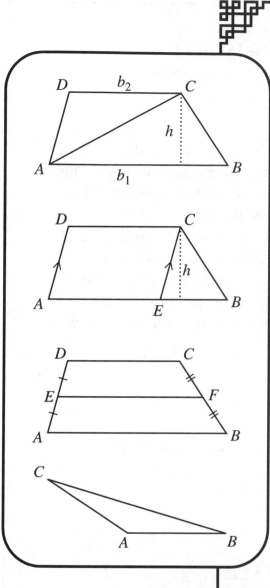

Exercises: Dissection

1. Find the formula for the area of a trapezoid in three ways: by dissecting along a diagonal, through its bases, and along its median. Refer to the first three diagrams on the left.

2. Sketch an obtuse triangle like the one on the bottom at left. Apply the dissection procedure to show that the sum of the interior angles in an obtuse triangle is 180 degrees.

3. Use the figure on page 34 to show that the area of a triangle is one-half the product of its base and altitude.

4. Show that the area of a rhombus is one-half the product of its diagonals.

5. Show that the area of a regular pentagon is one-half the product of its apothem and perimeter.

Inscribed Square Theorem

The *Jiuzhang suanshu (Nine Chapters of Mathematical Art)* is China's oldest mathematical text and it's the most important one from ancient times. This classic text was started in the Western Han dynasty and was completed in the early years of the Eastern Han dynasty (circa 50–100 A.D.), but it represents a mathematical tradition that echoes back to the period of the Zhou dynasty (founded during the eleventh century B.C.). It became the fundamental text on which subsequent Chinese mathematicians were to write commentaries. From the *Nine Chapters of Mathematical Art* comes the following geometrical theorem about the side of a square inscribed in any right triangle. Can you prove it?

The Theorem

The length of the side of a square inscribed in a right triangle is the quotient of the product and the sum of the legs.

Euclidean Form

Given: Right triangle *ABC* with inscribed square *CDEF*
$AC = b$; $BC = a$; $DC = s$

Prove: $s = \dfrac{ab}{a + b}$

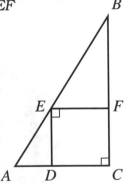

Liu Hui's Solution

Liu Hui was one of the great mathematicians of ancient China. He lived during the Three Kingdoms period when China was ruled by three separate monarchies (220–280 A.D.). Little is known about Liu Hui's personal life, but he lived in the northern kingdom of Wei. From his *Commentary on the Nine Chapters of Mathematical Art* (263 A.D.), Liu Hui provides us with the following creative solution to the inscribed square problem on page 36.

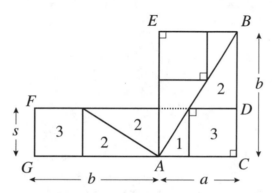

Liu Hui's figure with additional modern notation

In the figure, right triangle *ABC* with inscribed square is given. Duplicate right triangle *ABC* and rotate it to form rectangle *ACBE* with base *a* and altitude *b*.

Duplicate two triangles of region 2 and one square of region 3. Arrange the copies to form rectangle *CDFG* with base *a* + *b* and altitude *s*.

We define $A(R)$ as the area of region *R*. Give the reasons for the following algebraic steps.

1. $A(ACBE) = ab$

2. $A(CDFG) = A(ACBE)$

3. $A(CDFG) = s(a + b)$

4. $s(a + b) = ab$

5. $s = \dfrac{ab}{a + b}$ *Q.E.D.*

Western Solution

As a comparison to Liu Hui's solution for the inscribed square problem on page 36, we provide a typical modern Western approach based on Aristotle's principle that *the whole is equal to the sum of its parts*. The steps are outlined below. You are asked to supply the reasons.

Given: Right triangle ABC with inscribed square $CDEF$

$AC = b$; $BC = a$; $DC = s$

Prove: $s = \dfrac{ab}{a + b}$

$A(R) \equiv$ area of region R

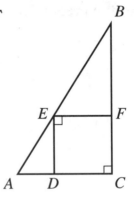

1. $A(\triangle ADE) + A(\triangle EFB) + A(\text{Sq. } CDEF) = A(\triangle ABC)$

2. $A(\triangle ADE) = \dfrac{a - s}{2} \cdot s = \dfrac{as - s^2}{2}$

3. $A(\triangle EFB) = \dfrac{b - s}{2} \cdot s = \dfrac{bs - s^2}{2}$

4. $A(\text{Sq. } CDEF) = s^2$

5. $A(\triangle ACB) = \dfrac{ab}{2}$

6. $\dfrac{as - s^2}{2} + \dfrac{bs - s^2}{2} + s^2 = \dfrac{ab}{2}$

7. $as - s^2 + bs - s^2 + 2s^2 = ab$

8. $as + bs = ab$

9. $s(a + b) = ab$

10. $s = \dfrac{ab}{a + b}$ $\quad$ Q.E.D.

From the Ancient Han Dynasty

Han Gaozu was the first emperor and founder of the Western Han dynasty (208 B.C.–8 A.D.). He reigned from 206 to 195 B.C. This period was impressive for the development of art, literature, and science as well as philosophy, political and social organization and the opening up of the Silk Road leading to commerce with the Roman Empire. From this time comes the *Jiuzhang suanshu (Nine Chapters of Mathematical Art)*, China's oldest mathematical text and its most important one from ancient times. From the *Nine Chapters of Mathematical Art* comes the following geometrical theorem about the diameter of a circle inscribed in any right triangle. Can you prove it?

Han Gaozu, based on a Ming painting

Inscribed Circle Theorem

The diameter of a circle inscribed in a right triangle is the quotient of twice the product of the legs and the sum of the three sides.

Euclidean Form

Given: Right triangle *ABC* with inscribed circle *O*
of diameter *d*; *AC* = *b*; *BC* = *a*; *AB* = *c*

Prove: $d = \dfrac{2ab}{a + b + c}$

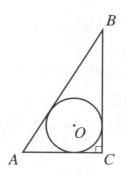

More from Liu Hui

Liu Hui provides another creative solution from his *Commentary on the Nine Chapters of Mathematical Art* (263 A.D.). We present his solution to the inscribed circle problem from page 39.

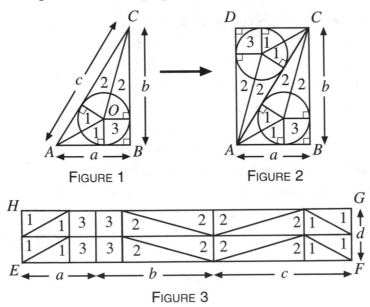

FIGURE 1   FIGURE 2

FIGURE 3

In Figure 1, right triangle *ABC* with inscribed circle is given. We have drawn the radii perpendicular to the sides of the triangle and two of the three segments between the center and the vertices of the triangle. The parts are labeled for convenience. The triangles marked as 1 are congruent, and so are the triangles marked as 2. (Can you prove it?)

Copy right triangle *ABC*. Rotate and translate the copy to form rectangle *ABCD* in Figure 2.

Double Figure 2 and rearrange the pieces using translation and rotation to make rectangle *EFGH* in Figure 3.

We define $A(R)$ as the area of region R. Give the reasons for the following algebraic steps.

1. $A(ABCD) = ab$

2. $A(EFGH) = 2ab$

3. $A(EFGH) = d(a + b + c)$

4. $d(a + b + c) = 2ab$

5. $d = \dfrac{2ab}{a + b + c}$ *Q.E.D.*

Western Solution

In contrast to Liu Hui's Chinese dissection solution for the inscribed circle problem on page 39, we provide a typical modern Western solution. Can you provide the reasons?

Given: Right triangle ABC with inscribed circle O
of diameter d; $AC = b$; $BC = a$; $AB = c$; $OP = r$

Prove: $d = \dfrac{2ab}{a + b + c}$

$\mathcal{A}(R) \equiv$ area of region R

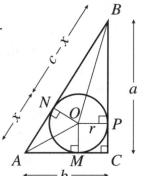

1. $\mathcal{A}(\text{Sq. } CMOP) + \mathcal{A}(\triangle AMO) + \mathcal{A}(\triangle ANO) + \mathcal{A}(\triangle BNO)$
   $+ \mathcal{A}(\triangle BPO) = \mathcal{A}(\triangle ABC)$

2. $r^2 + \dfrac{(AM)(r)}{2} + \dfrac{(AN)(r)}{2} + \dfrac{(BN)(r)}{2} + \dfrac{(BP)(r)}{2} = \dfrac{ab}{2}$

3. But $AM = b - r$; $AN = x$; $BN = c - x$; $BP = a - r$

4. $r^2 + \dfrac{(b - r)r}{2} + \dfrac{xr}{2} + \dfrac{(c - x)r}{2} + \dfrac{(a - r)r}{2} = \dfrac{ab}{2}$

5. $2r^2 + br - r^2 + xr + cr - xr + ar - r^2 = ab$

6. $br + cr + ar = ab$

7. $r(a + b + c) = ab$

8. $r = \dfrac{ab}{a + b + c}$

9. But $d = 2r$

10. $d = \dfrac{2ab}{a + b + c}$ Q.E.D.

The Measure of Heaven

China's oldest book, combining mathematics with astronomy, is the *Zhoubi suanjing (Zhou Dynasty Computation with the Gnomon)*, finalized during the first century A.D. The two scholars Chen Zi and his student Rong Fang discuss the movements of the sun. Their conversation leads to the problem of calculating the height of the sun above the earth. Although the astronomy at that time was based on the assumption that the earth was flat, their solution demonstrates how ancient Chinese mathematicians used dissection to solve problems with right triangles. The problem, using modern algebraic notation, is defined below and on page 43 with the accompanying Figure 1. Can you derive this formula?

The Problem

The sun at point A is directly over point C on the earth. Rays of light strike two vertical poles, or *gnomon*, of equal height h at locations S and T. They are a distance d apart. At the same time of day, the shadow lengths of the poles are recorded as $s_1 = SG$ and $s_2 = TB$. Show that $H = AC$, the height of the sun above the earth, is given by the formula

$$H = \frac{hd}{(s_2 - s_1)} + h$$

Below.

Ancient Chinese gnomon tower used to measure the shadows cast by the sun. This drawing is adapted from Joseph Needham's *Science and Civilisation in China*, vol. 3, plate XXXI.

Definitions for Measure of Heaven Problem

$H = AC$, height of sun above earth

$d = ST$, distance between poles

$s_1 = SG$, shadow length at first pole

$s_2 = TB$, shadow length at second pole

$h = ES = FT$, height of pole, or gnomon

S, location of first pole

T, location of second pole

G, first viewing point

B, second viewing point

Below.

Ancient Chinese surveyors with measuring pole, plumb line, and counting board.

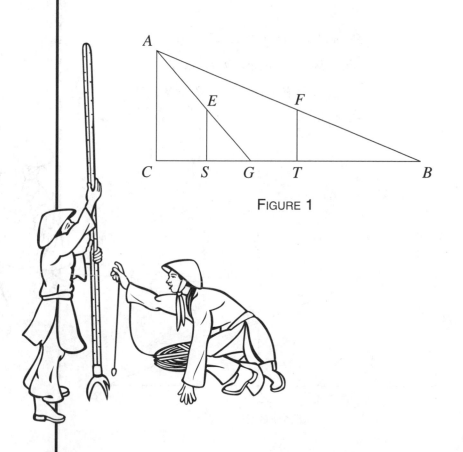

FIGURE 1

How High Is the Sun?

To derive the formula for the height of the sun above the earth on page 42, we use the Chinese dissection method. In Figure 2 below, we impose a rectangular grid of lines over the diagram of Figure 1 and label it as shown. The properties are summarized in the given. Take note of the fact that *FI* is added to the figure so that *FI* is parallel to *EG*. The steps are outlined on page 45. Think carefully through them and justify each step.

Given: $\overline{PN} \parallel \overline{BC}$ through E, K, F, J

$\overline{AM} \parallel \overline{BC}$ through Q, U, L, W

$\overline{PN} \perp \overline{QS}$; $\overline{PN} \perp \overline{UG} \perp \overline{LT}$; $\overline{PN} \perp \overline{WI}$

$\overline{FI} \parallel \overline{EG}$.

Below.

Ancient Chinese surveyor with measuring square.

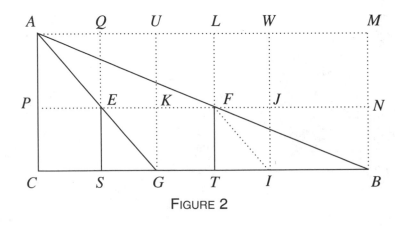

FIGURE 2

Proof

1. Define $A(PESC)$, $A(QUKE)$, $A(LWJF)$, $A(PFTC)$, $A(LMNF)$ as the areas of the regions defined by the vertices inside the parentheses.

2. $A(PESC) = A(QUKE) = A(LWJF)$

3. $A(PFTC) = A(LMNF)$

4. $A(PFTC) - A(PESC) = A(LMNF) - A(LWJF)$

5. $A(EFTS) = A(WMNJ)$

6. But $A(EFTS) = hd$ and $A(WMNJ) = (AP)(JN)$

7. $hd = (AP)\,(JN)$

8. But $JN = s_2 - s_1$

9. $hd = (AP)\,(s_2 - s_1)$

10. $AP = \dfrac{hd}{(s_2 - s_1)}$

11. $H = \dfrac{hd}{(s_2 - s_1)} + h$

$Q.E.D.$

Below.

Ancient Chinese surveyor with sighting board.

The Sea Island

The *Jiuzhang suanshu (Nine Chapters of Mathematical Art)* is China's oldest book on mathematics. In 263 A.D., Liu Hui wrote a famous commentary on it in which he added nine problems on the topic of surveying. His methods became the basis of Chinese surveying for the next 1,000 years. So important were the nine problems considered that they were made into a separate book at the beginning of the Tang dynasty (618–907 A.D.) The book was given the title *Haidao suanjing (Sea Island Canon of Mathematics)* because the very first problem required a distant observer to determine the size and distance of an island from the seashore.

The Problem

There is a sea island an unknown distance from the seashore. Someone wants to know how far away the island is and how high is its mountain peak. An observer erects two 30 ft poles 1,000 ft apart so that the mountain peak and the two poles are aligned. When the observer steps back 123 ft from the first pole, he sights the mountain peak from the ground; the top of the pole and the mountain peak align. When the observer steps back 127 ft from the second pole, he makes another sighting of the summit of the mountain so that the top of the second pole and the mountain peak align as viewed from the ground.

The solution begins on page 47.

Sea Island Solution

To solve the problem, refer to Figure 1 below. We shall use modern algebraic notation, but you should use the classical dissection approach of ancient China. Unlike the original problem, we shall obtain a general formula into which you can substitute the specific numbers. Use the definitions below and superimpose a rectangular grid on Figure 1 as shown in Figure 2 on page 48. Label the points accordingly. Justify each step of the proof.

Definitions

$D = SC$, distance to sea island

$H = AC$, height of mountain peak above sea level

$d = ST$, distance between poles

$s_1 = SG$, distance between pole and first observation

$s_2 = TB$, distance between pole and second observation

$h = ES = FT$, height of pole

S, location of first pole

T, location of second pole

G, first viewing point

B, second viewing point

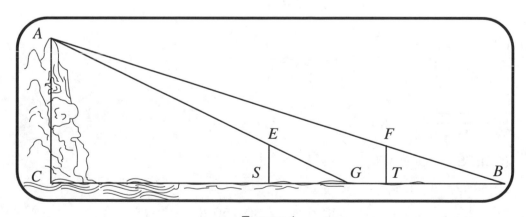

FIGURE 1

Given: $\overline{PN} \parallel \overline{BC}$ through E, K, F, J

$\overline{AM} \parallel \overline{BC}$ through Q, U, L, W

$\overline{PN} \perp \overline{QS}; \overline{PN} \perp \overline{UG}; \overline{PN} \perp \overline{LT}; \overline{PN} \perp \overline{WI}$

$\overline{FI} \parallel \overline{EG}.$

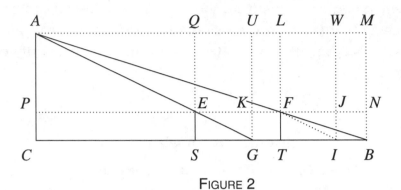

FIGURE 2

Proof

1. Define $\mathcal{A}(PESC)$, $\mathcal{A}(QUKE)$, $\mathcal{A}(LWJF)$, $\mathcal{A}(PFTC)$, $\mathcal{A}(LMNF)$ as the areas defined by the vertices inside the parentheses.

2. $\mathcal{A}(PESC) = \mathcal{A}(QUKE) = \mathcal{A}(LWJF)$

3. $\mathcal{A}(PFTC) = \mathcal{A}(LMNF)$

4. $\mathcal{A}(PFTC) - \mathcal{A}(PESC) = \mathcal{A}(LMNF) - \mathcal{A}(LWJF)$

5. $\mathcal{A}(EFTS) = \mathcal{A}(WMNJ)$

6. But $\mathcal{A}(EFTS) = hd$ and $\mathcal{A}(WMNJ) = (AP)(JN)$

7. $hd = (AP)(JN)$

8. But $JN = s_2 - s_1$

9. $hd = (AP) (s_2 - s_1)$

10. $AP = \dfrac{hd}{(s_2 - s_1)}$

11. $H = \dfrac{hd}{(s_2 - s_1)} + h$

12. $(CS)(ES) = (SG)(AP)$

13. But $CS = D$, $ES = h$, $SG = s_1$

14. $D = \dfrac{d \cdot s_1}{(s_2 - s_1)}$ $H = 7{,}530$ ft; $D = 30{,}750$ ft

Ancient Chinese Philosophy

Ancient Chinese teachers from the Zhou dynasty (1045–246 B.C.) said that there were two complementary principles in nature: the *Yin* and the *Yang*. Yin and Yang are usually understood as deriving out of the formless, unitary Dao (Tao), so it is the Dao that is the origin of all things. Yin and Yang are "complementary," rather than "opposing," for there is Yin in Yang and Yang in Yin. It is the ethereal material energy or force (*qi*) that actually composes things in the universe, whereas Yin and Yang can be understood as the "principles" of things— although "principle" was not a term used in the Zhou dynasty. The symbol for the yin-yang is shown in the figure at left.

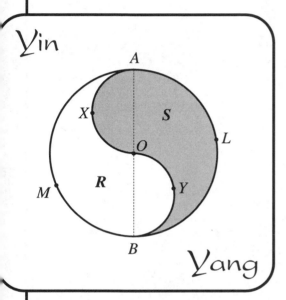

Yin

Yang

Yin-Yang Problem

In the figure, arc (*AXO*) and arc (*OYB*) form semicircles with diameters equal to the radius of circle *O*. Two interesting mathematical properties can be shown: (1) the area of region *R* equals the area of region *S*; (2) the length of the curved path from *A* to *B* through points *X*, *O*, and *Y* equals one-half the circumference of the circle *O*. The basic definitions follow with a geometric proof for you to complete on page 50.

Definitions

1. Let $A(R)$, $A(S)$ be the areas of regions *R* and *S*, respectively.

2. Let $A(AXO)$, $A(OYB)$, $A(ALB)$, and $A(AMB)$ be the areas of respective semi-circles.

3. Let $L(AXO)$ and $L(OYB)$ be defined as arc lengths of respective semicircles. $L(AXOYB)$ is the length of the curved path from *A* to *B* through points *X*, *O*, and *Y*.

Yin-Yang Proof

Given (Statements)	Prove (Reasons)
1. Circle *O* with diameter *AB*; semicircles *AXO* and *OYB* with diameters equal to $\dfrac{AB}{2}$.	1.
2. $A(S) = A(AXO) + A(ALB) - A(OYB)$; $A(R) = A(OYB) + A(AMB) - A(AXO)$	2.
3. $A(AXO) = A(OYB)$; $A(ALB) = A(AMB)$	3.
4. $A(R) = A(AXO) + A(ALB) - A(OYB)$	4.
5. $A(S) = A(R)$ *Q.E.D.*	5.
6. $L(AXOYB) = L(AXO) + L(OYB)$	6.
7. $L(AXO) = \pi\dfrac{AB}{4}$; $L(OYB) = \pi\dfrac{AB}{4}$	7.
8. $L(AXOYB) = \pi\dfrac{AB}{4} + \pi\dfrac{AB}{4}$	8.
9. $L(AXOYB) = \dfrac{\pi}{2}(AB)$	9.
10. $L(AXOYB) = \dfrac{1}{2}(\text{circumference})$	10.

       Q.E.D.

More Yin-Yang!

Given: Circle *O* with diameter *AD* containing points *A, B, C, D* such that *AB* = *BC* = *CD*;

semicircles: *AXB; AYC; BHD; CID.*

Prove: $A(R) = A(S) = A(T)$;

$L(AXBHD) = L(AYCID)$.

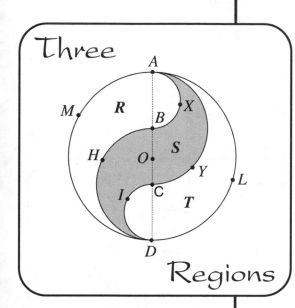

Three

Regions

Instructions

1. Study the Three Regions Yin-Yang figure, what is given, and what you need to prove in the problem. Use the suggestions that follow to help you construct a proof.

2. State the formulas for the area and circumference of a circle.

3. Develop a set of algebraic steps from the *given* to the *prove*.

4. Translate the algebraic steps into a formal proof by asking yourself for the reasons in each step.

5. Decide whether you need any additional theorems or definitions between steps. Supply the needed steps in your proof.

Another Case of Yin-Yang!

Given: Circle O with diameter AD containing points A, B, C, D such that $AB = OB = OC = CD$;

semicircles: AXB; AYO; AZC; CJD; OID; BHD.

Prove: $A(R) = A(S) = A(T) = A(U)$;
$L(AXBHD) = L(AYOID)$
$= L(AZCJD)$.

Instructions

1. Study the Four Regions figure, what is given, and what you need to prove in the problem. Use the suggestions that follow to help you construct a proof.

2. State the formulas for the area and circumference of a circle. Apply the formulas to the four paths and the four regions of area.

3. Develop a set of algebraic steps from the *given* to the *prove*.

4. Translate the algebraic steps into a formal proof by asking yourself for the reasons in each step.

5. Decide whether you need any additional theorems or definitions between steps. Supply the needed steps in your proof.

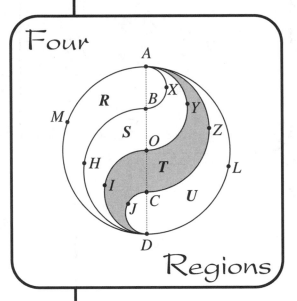

Four Regions

General Yin-Yang!

Given: Circle O with diameter AD containing points A, P, D;

semicircles: AXP; PYD.

Prove: $\llcorner(AXPYD) = \frac{1}{2}\pi(AD)$

Instructions

Study the Arbitrary Point figure, what is given, and what you need to prove in the problem. When you write the formulas for the semicircular arc lengths, use AP and PD as the diameters that define the semicircles AXP and PYD, respectively.

Arbitrary

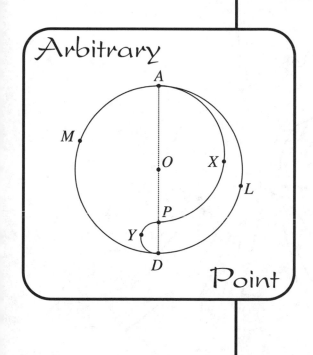

Point

Zhou Computation

From the *Zhoubi suanjing (Zhou Computation with the Gnomon)* ring the ancient words of the sage Duke of Zhou to his learned advisor Shang Gao. The duke asks, "How is it possible to measure the heavens and establish the calendar? What is the source of the numbers used to make such measurements?"

Shang Gao answers that number measure comes from the geometry of the circle and the square. He impresses his duke by placing bamboo sticks on a counting board to form the three diagrams shown on page 55. Deeply awed by what he sees, the Duke of Zhou exclaims: "Ah! Mighty is the art of numbers!"

Can you discover what mathematical properties so stirred the feelings of the duke?

Note.

The Zhou was an ancient kingdom that ruled China from 1045 to 246 B.C. In the *Zhoubi suanjing,* we find reference to this powerful dynasty in the person of the Duke of Zhou. However, the origins of the *Zhoubi suanjing* are shrouded in mystery. The final form of this book on ancient mathematics and astronomy traces back to the Western Han dynasty before the first century A.D.

Zhoubi Figures

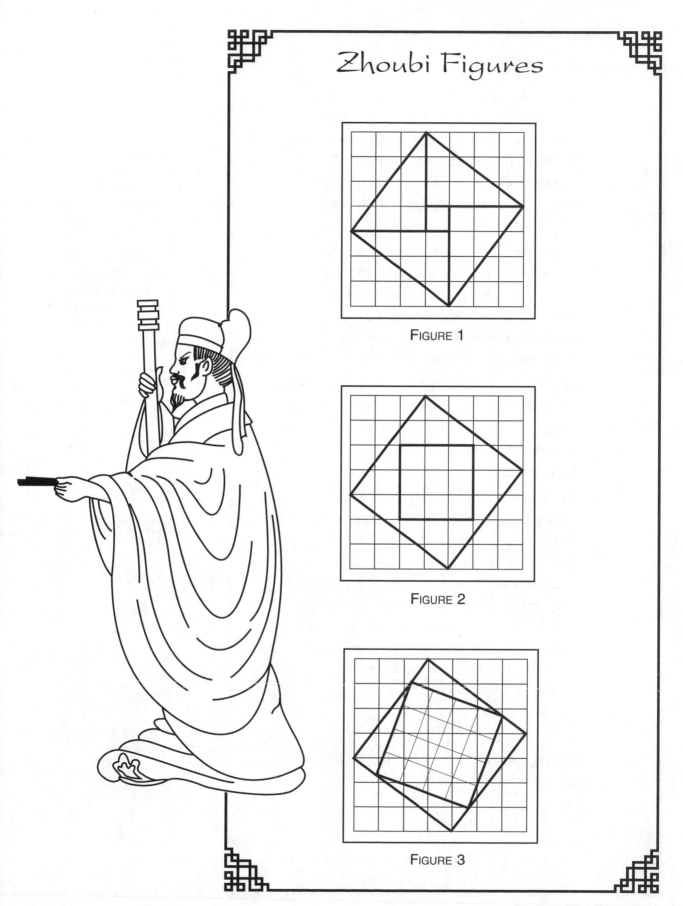

FIGURE 1

FIGURE 2

FIGURE 3

Zhou Exercise

1. Study the Zhou diagrams in the figures on page 55. In each diagram, assume that each of the square grids, underlying the bold-lined patterns, consists of unit squares. Explore possible numerical relations for the lengths and areas of the figures.

2. In Figure 1, find the length and area of the square-board grid and various bold-lined geometrical shapes on the board. Write down any numerical relationships that satisfy the Pythagorean theorem.

3. In Figure 2, can you find any geometrical relationships between the two bold-lined squares? Are there any numerical relationships that satisfy the Pythagorean theorem?

4. In Figure 3, the smaller bold-lined square is inscribed in the larger one. Find the numerical relationships between the sides and areas of the geometrical shapes formed on the board. Use the Pythagorean theorem and the quadratic formula to find the lengths of the legs of any of the four congruent right triangles formed between the two bold-lined squares.

Hint

Let one leg be defined as having length x and the other leg $5 - x$.

Below.

Shang dynasty stone column with symbols for heaven and earth (Shang dynasty, circa 1500–1045 B.C.).

From ancient times, the numbers 3, 4, and 5 have had important religious significance in China. The number 3 is a symbol for heaven, and the number 4 represents the earth. The number 5 is significant because it is the number of the Five Phases: Wood, Fire, Earth, Metal, and Water.

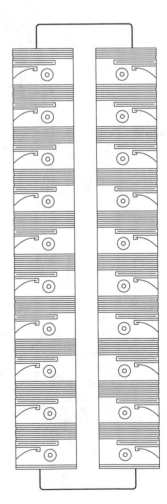

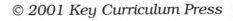

Gou-Gu Theorem

On page 55, we presented the three mathematical figures of Shang Gao. Figure 1 demonstrates the *Gou-gu* theorem, the Chinese version of the Pythagorean theorem. In ancient China, *Gou-gu* referred to the properties of right-angled triangles. *Gou* referred to the base of a right triangle (horizontal leg), while *Gu* signified vertical measure—the altitude of the triangle (vertical leg). The hypotenuse of the right triangle is called *xian*, or "bow string." The *Gou-Gu* theorem states that in a right triangle, the sum of the squares of the *Gou* and the *Gu* is equal to the square of the *xian*. Here is the diagram of the third-century Chinese commentator of the *Gou-Gu* theorem, Liu Hui:

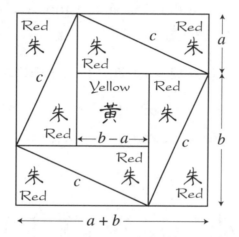

If we examine the figure without moving the pieces, it is clear that the square of side *c* has area equal to the sum of the areas of one yellow square and four red triangles. Using modern algebra, we write

$$c^2 = (b - a)^2 + 4R \qquad R = \frac{ab}{2} \qquad (1)$$

which simplifies to the familiar $a^2 + b^2 = c^2$.

Another way to look at the above figure is to think of the area of the large square with side $a + b$ as the sum of areas of the yellow square and four rectangles of base *a* and altitude *b*. Again, using algebra, we write

$$(a + b)^2 = (b - a)^2 + 4ab \qquad (2)$$

Equation (2) was used in ancient China to solve certain quadratic equations.

Liu Hui's Proof

In Liu Hui's third-century *Commentary on the Jiuzhang suanshu*, we find the *Gou-Gu* theorem in a form similar to that of the Pythagorean theorem:

In a right triangle, the area of the square on the hypotenuse (*xian*) equals the sum of the areas of the squares on the base (*gou*) and the altitude (*gu*). (See Figure 1.)

Lui Hui provides a simple proof based on the Chinese dissection process using Figure 2. We have shaded the right triangle having legs a and b and hypotenuse c. Start with square *ABCD* whose side is c and area is c^2. Remove pieces 1, 2, and 3 by translation and rotation to form pieces 4, 5, and 6, respectively. The original square has now been transformed into two new squares: (1) square *EFBG* of side b and area b^2; (2) square *GHIC* of side a and area a^2. We write

$$\mathcal{A}(GHIC) + \mathcal{A}(EFBG) = \mathcal{A}(ABCD)$$

$$a^2 + b^2 = c^2$$

Can you prove that pieces 1, 2, and 3 are congruent to pieces 4, 5, and 6, respectively?

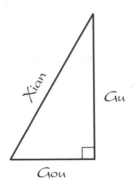

$$(Gou)^2 + (Gu)^2 = (Xian)^2$$

FIGURE 1

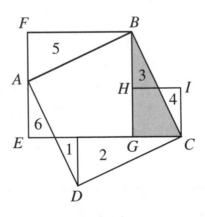

FIGURE 2

The Ambitious Horse

Character for Song

Yang Hui was one of the great medieval mathematicians of China. He lived during the Southern Song dynasty (1127–1279). As did many other great Chinese scholars, he wrote a commentary on the ancient Han classic *Nine Chapters of Mathematical Art*. From Yang Hui's *Xiangjie jiuzhang suanfa (Analysis of Arithmetical Rules in Nine Sections)*, published in 1261, we have the problem of the "ambitious horse." Can you solve this problem?

The Problem

An ambitious horse travels 193 Chinese miles (*li*) on the first day of a journey. Thereafter, the horse increases the distance traveled by 15 *li* each day. What is the total distance traveled, if the trip takes 15 days?

Ambitious Horse Solution

This problem can be readily solved using the formula for the sum of a finite arithmetic series:

$$S_n = a + (a + d) + (a + 2d) + \cdots + (a + (n - 1)d)$$

where a is the first term, n is the number of terms, and d is the constant difference. It can be shown that

$$S_n = \frac{n}{2}(a + a_n) \text{ and } a_n = a + (n - 1)d \qquad (1)$$

where a_n is the nth or last term of the series. In the problem, $a = 193$ *li*, $n = 15$, and $d = 15$. Hence, $a_n = 403$ and $S_n = 4{,}470$ *li*.

Yang Hui's Method

The Chinese solution makes use of Yang Hui's diagram (Figure 1). Each bar represents the distance the horse traveled on a particular day. The diagram is abbreviated in that five bars represent all fifteen bars or terms of an arithmetic series. The area of the entire figure represents the total distance the horse traveled on the journey. The area in Figure 1 is equivalent to that of the triangle and rectangle shown in Figure 2 on page 61. Using algebraic notation, we find the distance the horse traveled by combining the areas of the triangle and the rectangle in Figure 2:

$$S_n = A_1 + A_2, \text{ where } A_1 = \frac{1}{2}(a_n - a)(n) \text{ and } A_2 = an$$

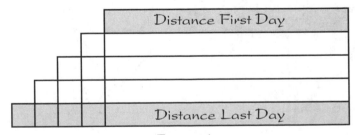

FIGURE 1

Equivalent Chinese and Western Solutions

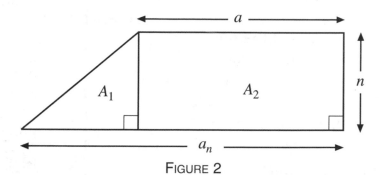

FIGURE 2

$$S_n = A_1 + A_2 = \frac{1}{2}(a_n - a)n + an$$

$$S_n = \frac{na_n - an}{2} + an$$

$$S_n = \frac{na_n - an + 2an}{2}$$

$$S_n = \frac{na_n + an}{2}$$

$$S_n = \frac{n}{2}(a + a_n) \qquad (2)$$

Thus, Equation (2) derived by the Chinese method is the same as Equation (1) derived by the Western formula. The Chinese geometric method is equivalent to the Western solution.

Ancient Square Root

Chinese mathematicians of the early Han dynasty (circa 200 B.C.) were proficient in extracting square roots. So ingenious were their methods that they led to the solution of quadratic equations and polynomial equations of higher degree.

The ancient Chinese method of extracting square roots relies on division and estimation, similar to algorithms of modern Western mathematics. However, in the Chinese technique, a strong component of geometry clarifies the mechanical steps. Since these steps were done on a calculating board with calculating rods, the theory can be better understood if algebra is used.

The fundamental principle of extracting square roots, in ancient Chinese and modern Western mathematics, can be explained by the two algebraic identities:

$$(a + b)^2 = a^2 + 2ab + b^2 \qquad (1)$$

$$(a + b + c)^2 = (a + b)^2 + 2(a + b)c + c^2 \qquad (2)$$

Equations (1) and (2), along with an iteration process, govern the extraction of square root of any rational number. The following explanation presents the principles of square root extraction in modern Western format, supplemented by the Chinese geometric dissection process. Fundamentally, the two processes are the same: one done on a calculating board, the other by written arithmetic.

Below.

Han dynasty books consisted of vertical writing on bamboo slips about 23.1 cm in length. As the drawing shows, the bundle could be rolled up and tied for convenience.

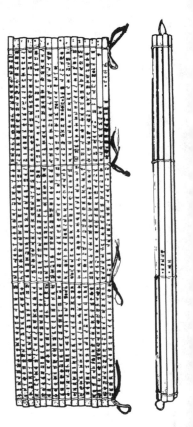

Square Root with Two Digits

Assume n represents a whole number whose positive square root is precisely a two-digit number $a + b$, where a is the value of the tens digit and b is the value of the ones digit. Our task is to derive $a + b$ from n.

Since $a + b$ is the square root of n, $n = a^2 + 2ab + b^2$. In Chinese mathematics, this fact was represented geometrically (see Figure 1). The area of the large square represents n, and the side of this square is $a + b$ or $\sqrt{n}$. Each of the cells of Figure 1 relates to the expression $a^2 + 2ab + b^2$.

There are two square cells of area a^2 and b^2, respectively; and there are rectangular cells of length a and width b, having a total area of $2ab$. As we explore the steps in extracting $a + b$ using the written algebraic process, we can see the steps unfold geometrically through the Chinese dissection process.

$$n = (a + b)^2 = a^2 + 2ab + b^2$$

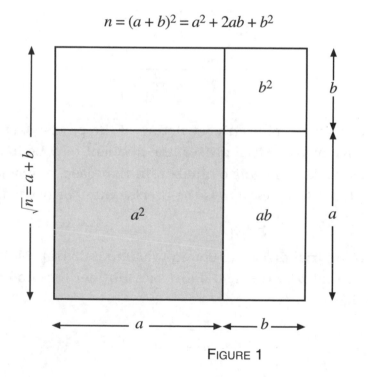

$$2ab \le n - a^2$$
$$b \le \frac{n - a^2}{2a}$$

FIGURE 1

Step 1

Set the number $n = a^2 + 2ab + b^2$ as the dividend. Find the principal square root of the first term and subtract its square from the dividend.

$$
\begin{array}{ll}
a & \longleftarrow \text{ Partial root} \\
\overline{\left| a^2 + 2ab + b^2 \right.} & \longleftarrow \text{ Dividend} \\
\underline{a^2} & \\
2ab + b^2 & \longleftarrow \text{ Remainder}
\end{array}
$$

In Figure 1 on page 63, this operation corresponds to finding the shaded square area a^2 and subtracting it from the area $(a + b)^2$ of the large square. The result, $2ab + b^2$, is the area of the L-shaped region called a *gnomon*.

Step 2

Estimate the second digit. Take twice a, the partial root, as a trial divisor. Divide the first term of the remainder. Write the quotient above the second term of the dividend.

$$
\begin{array}{ll}
& a \ + \ b \\
& \overline{\left| a^2 + 2ab + b^2 \right.} \\
& \underline{a^2} \\
\text{Trial divisor} \longrightarrow & 2a \,\big|\, 2ab + b^2
\end{array}
$$

When working with numerical values, the structure of the precise factors is unknown. So, when dividing by a trial divisor, the quotient may be too large so that the subtraction yields a negative number. In that case, a smaller quotient would be tested. In this case, b is the precise number needed.

Step 3

Add the quotient b to the trial divisor to obtain the actual divisor. Multiply the second term of the root b by the actual divisor. Subtract the product from the last remainder.

$$
\begin{array}{ll}
& a \ + \ b \\
& \overline{\left| a^2 + 2ab + b^2 \right.} \\
& \underline{a^2} \\
\text{Trial divisor} \longrightarrow & 2a \,\big|\, 2ab + b^2 \\
\text{Actual divisor} \longrightarrow & 2a + b \,\big|\, \underline{2ab + b^2} \\
& \qquad\qquad 0
\end{array}
$$

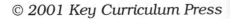

As previously mentioned, in working with numerical values, it is not always obvious what value to use for b. Re-examining the L-shaped gnomon of Figure 1 on page 63 reveals an important relationship Chinese mathematicians used to estimate b. By inspecting the relationship between the areas of the cells, it follows that

$$2ab \le 2ab + b^2$$

$$\text{But } 2ab + b^2 = n - a^2$$

$$2ab \le n - a^2$$

$$b \le \frac{n - a^2}{2a} \tag{3}$$

This formula provides the largest possible value of b as a trial number. After a is found, Formula (3) is easily evaluated since $n - a^2$ is the remainder in step 1. If the value of b is too large, the subtraction is negative and a smaller number must be tried.

Square Root with Three Digits

The process of extracting the square root of a number can be extended to a root with three or more digits. Assume n represents a whole number whose positive square root is precisely a three-digit number $a + b + c$, where a is the value of the hundreds digit, b is the value of the tens digit, and c is the value of the ones digit. We need to derive $a + b + c$, from n.

If $\sqrt{n} = a + b + c$, then $n = (a + b + c)^2$ by definition. Using Identity (2) on page 57 and expanding the terms, it follows that

$$(a + b + c)^2 = (a + b)^2 + 2(a + b)c + c^2$$

$$(a + b + c)^2 = a^2 + b^2 + c^2 + 2(ab + ac + bc) \tag{4}$$

Geometrically, Equation (4) can be represented by Figure 2 on page 66. The area of the large square represents $n = (a + b + c)^2$ with side equal to $\sqrt{n} = a + b + c$. Equation (4) conforms to the Chinese pattern of geometric dissection. The area of the large square is the sum of the areas of three squares and six rectangles as can be seen in the figure.

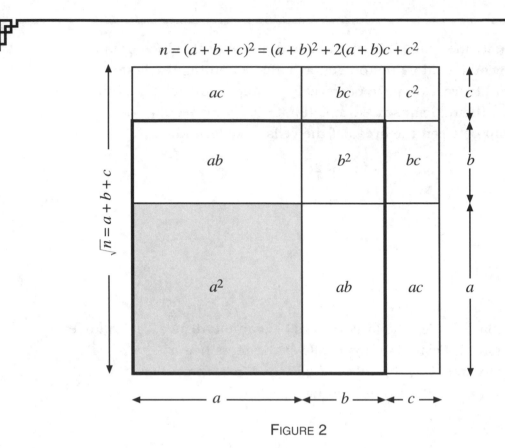

$$n = (a + b + c)^2 = (a + b)^2 + 2(a + b)c + c^2$$

FIGURE 2

In Figure 2, there is a square of side $a + b$ bounded by a heavier line for emphasis. This part of the figure is exactly like Figure 1 on page 63 except that a represents hundreds and b represents tens, instead of tens and ones, respectively. If the root extraction process for the two-digit case is applied to Figure 2, the heavier bounded square of Figure 2 corresponds to the shaded square of Figure 1. By treating the four cells as a single square in Figure 2, it has the same relationship with its outlining L-shaped gnomon as does the gnomon of Figure 1 with its shaded square.

The above described relationship is also seen between Equations (1) and (2) on page 62. Equation (2) has the same structure as Equation (1). If $a + b$ replaces a and c replaces b in Equation (1), Equation (1) becomes Equation (2). Thus, either from a geometric or algebraic point of view, we can determine the third digit as an iterated process of the two-digit case. In fact, we can extend the iterative process as many times as we wish to determine the square root of any rational number whose digits are finite. The following numerical example on page 67 can better illustrate the process.

Example

Find: $\sqrt{121,104}$

Step 1

Set 121,104 as the dividend, marking off the digits in pairs from right to left. The number of pairs is the same as the number of digits in the square root, in this case three.

$$12 \,{}'\, 11 \,{}'\, 04$$

Step 2

Examine the pair 12, representing 120,000. The largest whole-number square root contained in 12 is 3. The 3 is placed above the 12 as a partial square root and represents 300. The square of 3 is 9, but 9 actually represents $(300)^2$, or 90,000. We write 90,000 under the dividend and subtract, obtaining a remainder of 31,104.

```
        3
 ┌──────────────
 │ 12 ' 11 ' 04
 │  9   00   00
 └──────────────
    3   11   04
```

In most square root algorithms, 9 would be written under the 12 in abbreviated form, rather than its full place value of 90,000, but we wish to demonstrate the Chinese dissection process, showing the geometric regions corresponding to the numbers in the algorithm, beginning with Figure 3 on page 68.

In Figure 3, the number 121,104 is the area of square *ABCD*, while 90,000 is the area of shaded square *EFGD*. When the shaded area is removed from the figure, the L-shaped gnomon *ABCGFE* remains and has area equal to 31,104.

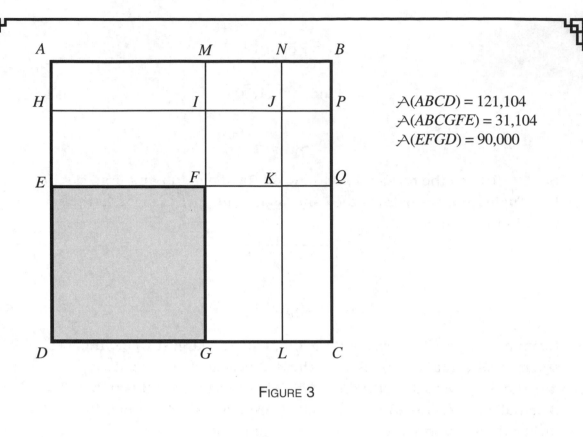

$A(ABCD) = 121,104$
$A(ABCGFE) = 31,104$
$A(EFGD) = 90,000$

FIGURE 3

Step 3

We are looking for the tens digit b in the root. With $a = 300$, and applying the Chinese formula, Equation (3) on page 65, with $b + c$ replacing b, we have

$$b + c \leq \frac{n - a^2}{2a}$$

$$b + c \leq \frac{31,104}{2(300)} \approx 51.8$$

Hence, the greatest possible value predicted for the tens digit is 50. Compute the area of gnomon *HJLGFE* with 50 as the value for b. The gnomon consists of two rectangles and a square (see Figure 4). This area is 32,500, an impossible value, since there was only 31,104 square units of area available. Hence, we need to try a smaller value for b. The next logical choice is $b = 40$.

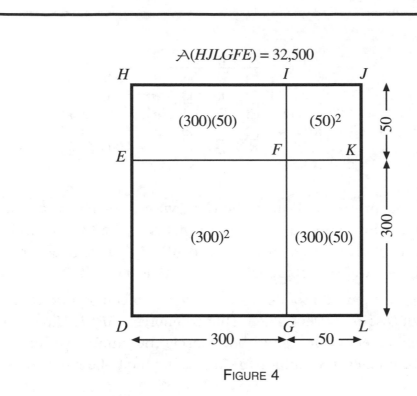

$$\mathcal{A}(HJLGFE) = 32{,}500$$

FIGURE 4

The corresponding steps of the algorithm in finding the tens digit b require that we first take twice the root and use this as a trial divisor. Divide the trial divisor into the remainder to get an estimate for the tens digit. Following this procedure, $31{,}104 \div 600 \approx 51.8$, which is exactly the same number obtained by the Chinese formula, Equation (3).

		3	5	← Partial trial root
		12 ' 11 ' 04		← Dividend
		9 00 00		← Square
Trial divisor →	2(300) = 600	3 11 04		← Remainder
Actual divisor →	600 + 50 = 650	3 25 00		← Trial product
		Impossible		← New remainder

As the above algorithmic steps demonstrate, 50 was an impossible value for the tens digit. We use 40 for our next choice. At the top of page 70, we repeat the algorithm with $b = 40$.

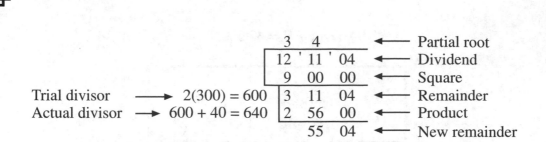

	3	4			
	12 ' 11 ' 04			←	Partial root
	9 00 00			←	Dividend
Trial divisor → 2(300) = 600	3 11 04			←	Square
Actual divisor → 600 + 40 = 640	2 56 00			←	Remainder
	55 04			←	Product
				←	New remainder

As this algorithmic process indicates, the value with $b = 40$ gives a new positive remainder. Since no larger value of b yields a positive remainder, we have found the correct value for the tens digit. At this stage of the algorithmic process, we have obtained a new partial root of 340.

In Figure 5, the new partial root 340 is the side of shaded square *HJLD* with area 115,600 square units. The L-shaped gnomon *ABCLJH* has area equal to the remainder, 5,504. Notice how closely the numbers of the Western algorithm follow the Chinese geometric method of dissection.

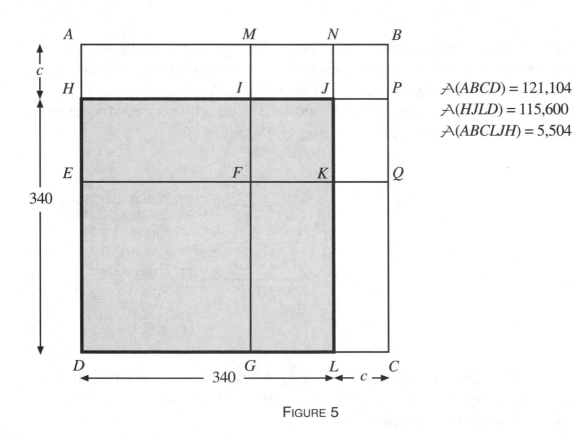

$\mathcal{A}(ABCD) = 121,104$
$\mathcal{A}(HJLD) = 115,600$
$\mathcal{A}(ABCLJH) = 5,504$

FIGURE 5

Step 4

We are looking for the ones digit c to complete the square root. In Figure 5 on page 70, c is the unknown side of the gnomon. If we can find a digit c that makes the gnomon have an area of exactly 5,504 square units, we will have found a square root of exactly three digits. If there were no ones digit c giving us the precise area of 5,504 square units, we could continue the iterations and find subsequent place values of tenths, hundredths, and so on, or resort to approximating the root with a fractional remainder.

Continuing our search for the ones digit c, we apply the Chinese estimation formula, Equation (3) on page 65, to Figure 6.

$$c \le \frac{n - (a + b)^2}{2(a + b)}$$

$$c \le \frac{5{,}504}{2(340)} \approx 8.09$$

The value of c cannot be greater than 8. If we use $c = 8$, the gnomon *ABCLJH* has area 5,504, and we have found the last digit of the square root. See Figure 6.

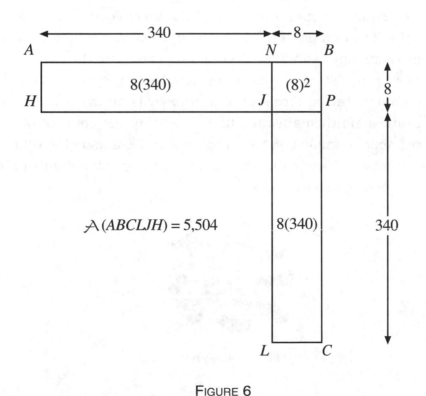

FIGURE 6

Returning to the corresponding steps of the algorithm, take twice 340 as the trial divisor to find *c*. Divide the trial divisor into the remainder to get the estimate for the ones digit. The result

$$5{,}504 \div 680 \approx 8.09$$

corresponds to the Chinese formula, Equation (3), we used when we looked at the geometric process. The final steps of the algorithm are written as

		3	4	8	← Square root
		12 ' 11 '	04		← Dividend
		9	00	00	← Square
	600	3	11	04	← Remainder
	640	2	56	00	← Product
Trial divisor →	2(340) = 680		55	04	← Remainder
Actual divisor →	680 + 8 = 688		55	04	← Product
				0	← Final remainder

By comparing step 4 and Figure 6 with step 3 and Figure 3, we see that the algorithmic steps or geometric procedure form an iteration process. Chinese mathematicians of the early Han dynasty were capable of extracting the square root of any rational number. They had a choice of continuing the iteration process to whatever place value they thought sufficient or using approximation formula to terminate the process. At this early period of history, a well-developed decimal system existed in China. Sometimes, the square root of a number is an irrational number. Although Chinese mathematicians did not develop the concept of irrational numbers completely, they recognized them as being different from other numbers. They called irrational numbers *side numbers* in the context of extracting square roots.

Han dynasty character

Quadratic Equations from the Han Dynasty

From the *Nine Chapters of Mathematical Art*, we learn that ancient Chinese mathematicians of the early Han dynasty solved quadratic equations of the form $x^2 + mx - n = 0$, where m and n are positive rational numbers. Their technique was based on geometrical dissection and the square root extraction process performed on the calculating board. In all Chinese examples, problems were numerically specific and did not have the benefit of a written algebra.

We can best understand the ancient Chinese method by outlining the process for a solution having a three-digit answer. However, this process generalizes to any rational number solution or irrational number, when used with the approximation formula for the remainder.

Suppose $x_1 = a + b + c$ is a positive root of Equation (1), where a is the hundreds digit, b is the tens digit, and c is the ones digit:

$$x^2 + mx - n = 0 \tag{1}$$

Substituting the root $x_1 = a + b + c$ into Equation (1), we have the following new Equation (2) involving the three digits of the root:

$$(a + b + c)^2 + m(a + b + c) - n = 0 \tag{2}$$

Equation (2) can be expanded and terms rearranged to be compatible with the Chinese square root extraction process:

$$(a + b + c)^2 = a^2 + b^2 + c^2 + 2(ab + ac + bc) + m(a + b + c) - n = 0 \tag{3}$$

Impression made from an early bronze seal belonging to a Han dynasty general.

Equation (1) has a special geometric relation to Figure 1 below. The area of square *AIJD* equals x^2. The area of the shaded rectangle *IBCJ* equals mx, and the area of rectangle *ABCD* equals n. Furthermore, Equation (1), as a whole, is a statement about the dissection process: When all the component rectangles are removed from rectangle *ABCD*, the area of rectangle *ABCD* is reduced to zero.

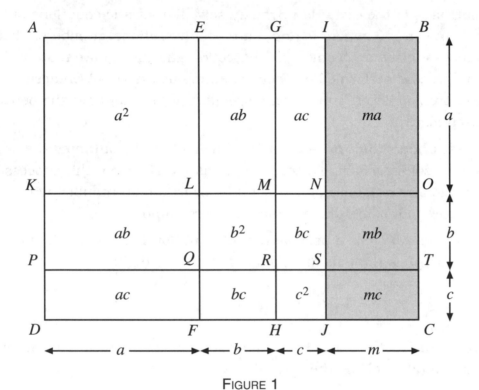

FIGURE 1

We begin solving Equation (1) by focusing our attention on Figure 1. The essential idea is to begin the process of extracting the square root on square *AIJD* with the value n = area of *ABCD*—not the area of square *AIJD* as in the case of a regular square root extraction. Keep in mind that calculating the square root this way has an element of trial and error. We are forcing the solution of the quadratic equation into the form of square root extraction. As we find a, b, and c through the square root process, we successively remove the parts of the shaded rectangles, that is, ma, mb, mc. These steps are outlined on the next page, followed by a numerical example.

Outline of Square Root Extraction

1. Determine a by finding the largest square of a contained in n.

2. Compute $a^2 + am$ and subtract from n. This removes square $AELK$ and rectangle $IBON$ from Figure 1.

3. Estimate b. It can be shown from Figure 1 that

$$b \leq \frac{n - a^2 - am}{2a + m} \tag{4}$$

   If b is chosen numerically too large, it will produce a negative remainder in step 4. Choose a smaller trial value for b and repeat the calculations.

4. Compute $2ab + b^2 + mb$ and subtract from the previous remainder $n - a^2 - am$. This corresponds to removing square $LMRQ$, rectangle $EGML$, rectangle $KLQP$, and rectangle $NOTS$ from Figure 1.

5. Estimate c. From Figure 1, it can be shown from the relationship between cells that

$$c \leq \frac{(n - a^2 - am)(2ab + b^2 + mb)}{2(a + b) + m} \tag{5}$$

6. Compute $c^2 + 2ac + 2bc + mc$ and subtract from the last remainder $(n - a^2 - am)(2ab + b^2 + mb)$. This corresponds to removing square $RSJH$, rectangle $GINM$, rectangle $NSRM$, rectangle $QRHF$, rectangle $PQFD$, and rectangle $STJC$.

Example

Solve $x^2 + 15x - 126{,}324 = 0$ for x. $\tag{6}$

Since the constant 126,324 has six digits, the square root of this number and Equation (6) are estimated as having three digits. We assume that $x = a + b + c$ is the form of the solution. We proceed using the modern Western form of the square root algorithm with some modifications. Equation (6) is set out geometrically for the Chinese dissection process as shown in Figure 2 on the next page.

$$x^2 + 15x - 126{,}324 = 0$$

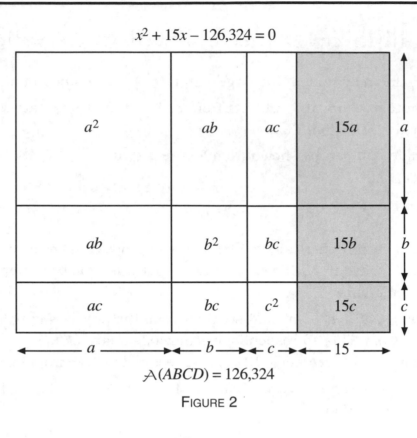

$$\mathcal{A}(ABCD) = 126{,}324$$

FIGURE 2

Step 1

Set 126,324 as the dividend. Find digit a and compute $a^2 + 15a$. Subtract the result from the dividend to obtain the first remainder.

$a = 300$
$a^2 = 90{,}000$
$15a = 4{,}500$
$a^2 + 15a = 94{,}500$

3				← Partial root
12 ' 63 ' 24				← Dividend
9	45	00		← $a^2 + 15a$
3	18	24		← First remainder

Step 2

Find b. By using Formula (4) on page 75, we estimate b. Accordingly, $b \le 51$. The value $b = 50$ is too large, so use $b = 40$. Then we compute the value of $2ab + b^2 + 15b$ and subtract from the first remainder. If $a = 300$ and $b = 40$, then $2ab + b^2 + 15b = 26{,}200$.

$$
\begin{array}{ccc}
3 & 4 & \\
\hline
12\ '\ 63\ '\ 24 & & \longleftarrow \text{ Partial root} \\
\end{array}
$$

3	4		← Partial root
12 ' 63 ' 24			← Dividend
9	45	00	← $a^2 + 15a$
3	18	24	← Remainder
2	62	00	← $2ab + b^2 + 15b$
	56	24	← New remainder

Step 3

Find *c*. By using Formula (5) on page 75, we estimate the value of *c*. Accordingly, if $a = 300$ and $b = 40$, $c \le 8.09$. We use $c = 8$ and compute $c^2 + 2ac + 2bc + 15c$ and subtract from the last remainder. If $a = 300$, $b = 40$, and $c = 8$, $c^2 + 2ac + 2bc + 15c = 5{,}624$. Since the final remainder is zero, $x = 348$ is the solution of the quadratic equation $x^2 + 15x - 126{,}324 = 0$.

3	4	8	← Final root
12 ' 63 ' 24			← Dividend
9	45	00	← $a^2 + 15a$
3	18	24	← First remainder
2	62	00	← $2ab + b^2 + 15b$
	56	24	← Second remainder
	56	24	← $c^2 + 2ac + 2bc + 15c$
		0	← Final remainder

If the last remainder of this process had not been zero, two additional zeros could have been added to the right of 24 in the dividend. The process can be extended along the established pattern to find the tenths place. There is no limit to this process, except perhaps fatigue. As many decimal place values as are needed can be obtained by adding more pairs of zeros to the right side of the dividend. If the root is irrational, the process can be terminated after reaching a desired accuracy. In such cases, the final place value can be approximated by remainder formula. Ancient Chinese mathematicians did not develop the concept of irrational number, but recognized that such nonterminating decimals were different and called them *side numbers*.

Advanced Mathematics of Medieval China

During the Song and Yuan dynasties (960–1368 A.D.), China developed an impressive amount of advanced mathematics. One of those achievements was the solution of polynomial equations of higher degree. As early as the mid-eleventh century, the illustrious Chinese mathematician Jia Xian introduced an iterated multiplication process on the calculating board for extracting roots or solving polynomial equations of arbitrary degree. His method was equivalent to the Ruffini-Horner method developed about 800 years later in Europe.

Since Jia Xian's work on solving polynomial equations was done on a calculating board with movable calculating rods, we can best understand his mathematics using modern algebraic techniques. The logical basis for justifying Jia Xian's method rests on the *diminished root theorem* from the part of algebra known as the *theory of equations.*

Diminished Root Theorem

Let $f(x) = a_o x^n + a_1 x^{n-1} + a_2 x^{n-2} + \cdots + a_n = 0$ be a rational integral polynomial defined over $x \in R$. For any $c \in R$, $f(x)$ is successively divided by $x - c$ as follows:

$Q_1(x)$ is the quotient and r_1 is the remainder of $f(x) \div (x - c)$;

$Q_2(x)$ is the quotient and r_2 is the remainder of $Q_1(x) \div (x - c)$;

$Q_3(x)$ is the quotient and r_3 is the remainder of $Q_2(x) \div (x - c)$;

and so on, until the process ends with $Q_n(x) = a_o$ and r_n.

If a new polynomial equation $f(y)$ is formed such that

$f(y) = a_o y^n + r_n y^{n-1} + r_{n-1} y^{n-2} + \dots + r_2 y + r_1 = 0$, then the roots of the $f(y) = 0$ equation are c less than those of the $f(x) = 0$ equation, that is, $y = x - c$.

A simple example of a type of problem encountered by Jia Xian was the extraction of a fourth root of a number or the solution of a fourth-degree polynomial equation. The two processes can be interchangeable as the following example illustrates.

Example 1

$$\text{Find } x = \sqrt[4]{279{,}841} \tag{3}$$

$$\text{or solve for } x, \ x^4 - 279{,}841 = 0 \tag{4}$$

At right.

Jia Xian was familiar with the binomial expansion diagram shown here. The European version known as Pascal's triangle was discovered 600 years later by the French mathematician Blaise Pascal (1623–1662).

The illustration shown was first published in Zhu Shijie's *Siyuan yujian xicao* in 1303.

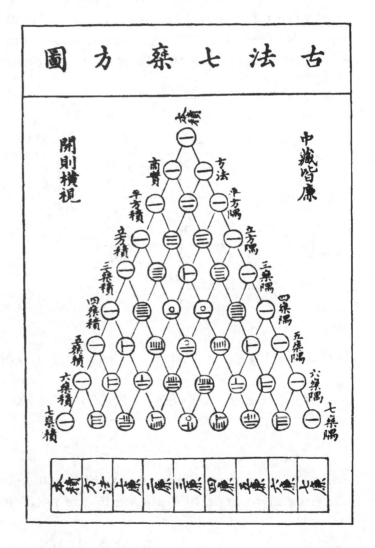

Solution

In Chinese mathematics, Equations (3) and (4) are equivalent as only a single positive root was sought for Equation (4).

In our solution to the problem, we apply the diminished root theorem to Equation (4) and use synthetic division to simplify the process.

Step 1

Our process begins by making an estimate. We know that $20 < x < 30$ because $(20)^4 < x^4 < (30)^4$. Assume that $x = 20 + y$, where $0 < y < 10$. This transformation implies that the solution x is at least 20 plus some positive number less than 10. If we apply the diminished root theorem to Equation (4) with $c = 20$, we obtain a new equation in y, whose solution is a number less than 10. Using synthetic division, we get

1	0	0	0	−279,841	20
	20	400	8,000	160,000	
1	20	400	8,000	**−119,841**	
	20	800	24,000		
1	40	1,200	**32,000**		
	20	1,200			
1	60	**2,400**			
	20				
1	**80**				

Therefore, if $y = x - 20$, the new equation in y is

$$g(y) = y^4 + 80y^3 + 2{,}400y^2 + 32{,}000y - 119{,}841 = 0 \qquad (5)$$

Step 2

Since Chinese mathematics used only positive roots, we can assume that all terms involving y in Equation (5) are positive. Therefore,

$$32{,}000y - 119{,}841 \le 0 \qquad (6)$$

$$y \le 3.7$$

Accordingly, $y \le 3.7$ can be used to approximate the next digit of the root. We use $y = 3$ as an approximation for the ones digit of the root. Applying the diminished root theorem to Equation (5), we set up the transformation $y = z + c$, where $c = 3$, to find a new equation in z whose solution we anticipate to have a value in the tenths place, that is, $z < 1$.

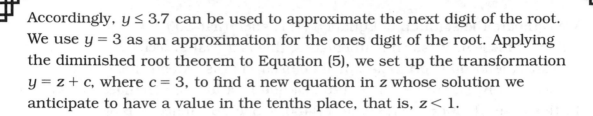

	80	2,400	32,000	−119,841	3
1	3	249	7,947	119,841	
1	83	2,649	39,947	**0**	

Applying the diminished root theorem, we find that after the first synthetic division, the first remainder is zero. We need not continue to divide synthetically because the first division tells us that $g(3) = 0$. This fact follows by use of the remainder theorem of modern algebra: If $g(y) \div (y - c)$ has remainder r, then $g(c) = r$.

Since $y = 3$ is the solution of Equation (5) and $y = x - 20$, it follows by substitution that $x = 23$ is the solution to Equations (3) or (4). Thus we found that 23 is the fourth root of 279,841 or $x = 23$ is the solution of the polynomial equation $x^4 - 279,841 = 0$.

This first example was intended to be very simple to illustrate the basic process of solving higher-degree polynomials. As a second example that is more typical of using the diminished root theorem and Jia Xian's method, we return to the Quadratic Equation (6) on page 75, where we solved the equation using the geometric dissection method of the Han dynasty. It is interesting to compare the numerical values generated between the two processes.

Example 2

Solve $x^2 + 15x - 126{,}324 = 0$ for x.

Step 1

We write the equation in functional notation to better communicate the reasoning:

$$\text{Solve } f(x) = x^2 + 15x - 126{,}324 = 0 \text{ for } x. \tag{1}$$

We estimate the solution of Equation (1) is such that $300 < x < 400$. In either Chinese or Western mathematics, this is a trial process. In modern algebra, the *location principle* would be used, that is, substitute arbitrary values of x in $f(x) = x^2 + 15x - 126{,}324$ and look for sign changes in $f(x)$. In this case, $f(300) = -31{,}824$ and $f(400) = 39{,}676$. Hence, a root for Equation (1) falls between $x = 300$ and $x = 400$. The steps using synthetic division follow:

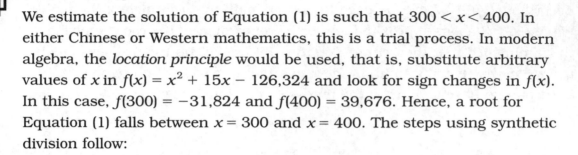

Location Principle

1	15	−126,324	⌐300
	300	94,500	
1	315	**−31,824**	

1	15	−126,324	⌐400
	400	166,000	
1	415	**+39,676**	

$$f(x) = x^2 + 15x - 126{,}324$$
$$f(300) = -31{,}824$$
$$f(400) = +39{,}676$$

Step 2

We apply the diminished root theorem to Equation (1) with $x = y + 300$, where $0 < y < 100$. In the transformation to the new equation in y, the solution, y, is reduced one place value.

1	15	−126,324	⌐300
	300	94,500	
1	315	**−31,824**	
	300		
1	**615**		

According to the diminished root theorem, we have the new equation in y with root reduced by 300:

$$g(y) = y^2 + 615y - 31{,}824 = 0 \qquad (2)$$

Step 3

Since $y^2 \geq 0$, Equation (2) can be used to make an estimate for the solution of y. We write the following inequality based on this assumption:

$$615y - 31{,}824 \leq 0 \qquad\qquad (3)$$

$$y \leq 51.7$$

Thus, by trial we determine that y is at least 40. Using the location principle, we have $g(50) = +1{,}426$ and $g(40) = -5{,}624$. The sign change between $y = 40$ and $y = 50$ implies that the solution for y is such that $40 < y < 50$. The steps using synthetic division follow:

1	615	−31,824	50
	50	33,250	
1	665	**+1,426**	

1	615	−31,824	40
	40	26,200	
1	655	**−5,624**	

$$g(y) = y^2 + 615y - 31{,}824$$
$$g(50) = +1{,}426$$
$$g(40) = -5{,}624$$

Step 4

We apply the diminished root theorem to Equation (2) with $y = z + 40$, where $0 < z < 10$. We obtain a new equation in z whose solution is 40 less than the solution of the equation in y. Applying the diminished root theorem using synthetic division, we have

1	615	−31,824	40
	40	26,200	
1	655	**−5,624**	
	40		
1	**695**		

Taking the values from the previous synthetic division, we can write the following new function in *z*:

$$h(z) = z^2 + 695z - 5624 = 0 \tag{4}$$

Since $z^2 \geq 0$, Equation (4) can be used to estimate the solution of *z*. We write the following inequality:

$$695z - 5624 \leq 0 \tag{5}$$

$$z \leq 8.09$$

Thus, by trial we determine that *z* is at least 8. We start by applying the location principle. We have $h(8) = 0$. There is no need to continue as we have found the exact solution for Equation (4). The steps are as follows:

Location Principle

1	695	−5,624	8
	8	5,624	
1	703	**0**	

$$h(z) = z^2 + 695z - 5{,}624$$
$$h(8) = 0$$

Since $z = 8$ and $y = z + 40$, then $y = 48$.

But $x = 300 + y$.

Therefore, $x = 348$ and is the solution of

$$f(x) = x^2 + 15x - 126{,}324 = 0.$$

We have used modern algebra and synthetic division to perform the steps of the solution of Quadratic Equation (1). Jia Xian and other medieval Chinese mathematicians used the calculating board. Although there were no permanent recorded steps during the process, the actual numbers on the calculating board correspond to the written numbers in our synthetic division steps.

Problem of the 100 Fowls

As early as the fifth century A.D., Chinese mathematicians solved problems with indeterminate solutions. We find the intriguing problem known as the "Problem of the One Hundred Fowls" in the Chinese classic *Zhang Qiujian suanjing (The Computational Classic of Zhang Qiujian)*. The problem follows, expressed in contemporary language. Can you find a solution?

The Problem

A rooster costs 5 copper coins called *qian*. A hen costs 3 *qian*, while three chicks can be purchased for 1 *qian*. You have 100 *qian* to buy exactly 100 fowls. How many roosters, hens, and chicks are there?

Hint

There are several possible solutions. Assume that the solution has at least one of each type of fowl.

Solution to the 100 Fowls Problem

Let: x be the number of roosters;

y be the number of hens;

z be the number of chicks.

Then: $x + y + z = 100$ (1)

$5x + 3y + \frac{1}{3}z = 100$ (2)

Solving Equation (1) for z and substituting into Equation (2), we have

$$5x + 3y + \frac{1}{3}(100 - x - y) = 100$$

$$y = 25 - \frac{7}{4}x \quad (3)$$

Equation (3) does not have a unique solution. Since any solution in x, y, and z must be a positive integer, we introduce the parameter a, $a \in N$ defined by

$$x = 4a \quad (4)$$

Substituting Equation (4) into Equation (3), we have

$$y = 25 - 7a \quad (5)$$

Substituting both Equations (4) and (5) into Equation (1), we have

$$z = 75 + 3a \quad (6)$$

Thus, we can redefine the equation set of (1) and (2) by the following parametric set in a.

$$x = 4a \quad (4)$$

$$y = 25 - 7a \quad (5)$$

$$z = 75 + 3a \quad (6)$$

The solution set in (x, y, z) is infinite. If $a = 0$, there can be no roosters. If $a = 1$, we have Zhang Qiujian's classic solution of 4 roosters, 18 hens, and 78 chicks. What other solutions are possible?

The Emperor of Qin Secretly Counts His Soldiers

Chinese mathematics had the capability of solving remainder problems or problems of simultaneous congruences very early in its history. From the *Sunzi suanjing (The Mathematical Book of Master Sun)*, these kinds of problems can be documented to the fourth or fifth century A.D. Later, in 1247, Qin Jiushao published his *Shushu jiuzhang (Computational Techniques in Nine Chapters)*. One popular version of Qin Jiushao's problems has the intriguing title "The Emperor of Qin Secretly Counts His Soldiers." The problem follows, expressed in contemporary language. Can you solve it?

The Problem

The Emperor of Qin secretly counts his soldiers in an enigmatic manner. When he counts his soldiers in groups of three, two soldiers are left. When the emperor counts in groups of five, three soldiers are left, and when the soldiers are counted in groups of seven, two soldiers are left. How many soldiers are there? What is the smallest number of soldiers possible?

Chinese Remainder Theorem

Solutions of problems such as "The Emperor of Qin Secretly Counts His Soldiers" were so prominent in the early history of Chinese mathematics that even Western historians refer to the basis of the method of solution as the *Chinese remainder theorem*. We utilize modern congruence notation of number theory to first state the Chinese remainder theorem and then apply it to the Emperor of Qin problem.

Definition:

$a \equiv b \pmod{m}$ if and only if $a = b + mk$, where a, b, k, and $m \in N$

Suppose x is an integer such that, when it is divided by m_1, the remainder is r_1. If x is divided by m_2, the remainder is r_2. If the process is repeated an arbitrary number of times, say k, the divisor of x is m_k, the remainder is r_k, m_k, $r_k \in N$. This process is equivalent to the following set of congruences:

$$x \equiv r_1 \pmod{m_1}$$

$$x \equiv r_2 \pmod{m_2}$$

$$x \equiv r_3 \pmod{m_3}$$

$$\vdots$$

$$x \equiv r_k \pmod{m_k} \tag{1}$$

If m_1, m_2, m_3, ..., m_k are pairwise relatively prime and $M = m_1 m_2 m_3 \ldots m_k$, then there exists a set of integers a_1, a_2, a_3, ..., a_k such that for each a_k,

$$a_k \frac{M}{m_k} \equiv 1 \pmod{m_k} \tag{2}$$

and

$$x \equiv a_1 r_1 \frac{M}{m_1} + a_2 r_2 \frac{M}{m_2} + \cdots + a_k r_k \frac{M}{m_k} \pmod{M} \tag{3}$$

Solution to the Emperor of Qin Problem

Let: x be the number of soldiers.

Then: $x \equiv 2 \pmod 3$ (4)

$x \equiv 3 \pmod 5$

$x \equiv 2 \pmod 7$

Applying the Chinese remainder theorem from page 88, we have

$$m_1 = 3 \qquad r_1 = 2 \qquad M = 3 \cdot 5 \cdot 7 = 105$$

$$m_2 = 5 \qquad r_2 = 3$$

$$m_3 = 7 \qquad r_3 = 2$$

The three values of a_k are defined by Equation (2) on page 88. It follows by substitution that

$$a_1 \frac{M}{m_1} = a_1 \frac{105}{3} = 35a_1 \equiv 1 \pmod 3 \tag{5}$$

$$a_2 \frac{M}{m_2} = a_2 \frac{105}{5} = 21a_2 \equiv 1 \pmod 5 \tag{6}$$

$$a_3 \frac{M}{m_3} = a_3 \frac{105}{7} = 15a_3 \equiv 1 \pmod 7 \tag{7}$$

Applying the definition of congruence to Equations (5), (6), and (7), it follows that $a_1 = 2$, $a_2 = 1$, $a_3 = 1$ satisfy the congruences. Substituting the values of a_k in Equation (3) on page 88, we have

$$x \equiv 2 \cdot 2 \cdot 35 + 1 \cdot 3 \cdot 21 + 1 \cdot 2 \cdot 15 \pmod{105}$$

$$x \equiv 23 \pmod{105}$$

Thus, 23 is the smallest number of soldiers. However, by adding integral multiples of 105 to 23, you can have additional solutions.

Pillar of Delightful Contemplation

Above.

The character for *Ming* of the Ming dynasty (1368–1644 A.D.).

Below.

Drawing based on a Ming dynasty painting.

The following problem from ancient China is based on the Han classic, the *Nine Chapters of Mathematical Art.*

The Problem

Resting on the floor of a pavillion is a cylindrical pillar 20 ft high and 3 ft in circumference. A floral pattern with a vine wraps uniformly about the pillar. One end of the vine-pattern starts at the base of the pillar and winds so that the other end just reaches to the very top of the pillar. Can you find the length of the vine wound about the pillar?

Hint

The ancient text of the *Nine Chapters of Mathematical Art* provides a rule that can help you solve the problem:

"Take seven times the circumference of the pillar for the second side of a right triangle and the pillar's height for the first side. The hypotenuse is the length of the vine."

What assumptions did the Chinese mathematicians make in using this method?

Solution to the Pillar of Delightful Contemplation Problem

Think of the pillar as being sliced horizontally by parallel planes so that seven congruent cylindrical parts are stacked together. Then each one of the cylindrical parts can be represented by Figure 1, with base diameter $3/\pi$ ft and altitude $20/7$ ft. The path of the vine starts at point A and winds uniformly to point B directly above the starting point. We designate the length of the path by x. (Figures are not drawn to scale.)

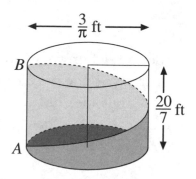

FIGURE 1

FIGURE 2

Next, cut the cylinder in Figure 1 along the path of the vine and unwind it into the plane right triangle of Figure 2. The base of the triangle equals the circumference of the cylinder, 3 ft. The altitude of the triangle is $20/7$ ft. Applying the Pythagorean theorem, we find the length of the vine for one turn as follows:

$$x^2 = (3)^2 + \left(\frac{20}{7}\right)^2 = 9 + \frac{400}{49} = \frac{841}{49}$$

$$x = \sqrt{\frac{841}{49}} = \frac{29}{7} \text{ ft}$$

In Figure 3, the seven turns of the vine are shown as a composite of seven right triangles, each with hypotenuse x. Therefore, the length of the entire vine is $7x$ or 29 ft.

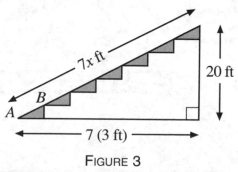

FIGURE 3

Pool of Celebrated Knowledge

The following problem from ancient China is based on the Han classic, the *Nine Chapters of Mathematical Art*.

The Problem

In a garden, there is a square pond 10 ft on a side. A reed grows in the very middle of the pond, with its top measuring 1 ft above the surface of the water. When the reed is drawn directly to any of the sides of the pond, its top touches the surface of the water. Assume that the pond has uniform depth. Find the depth of the water and the length of the reed.

Solution to the Pool of Celebrated Knowledge Problem

The solution of the problem is an application of the Pythagorean theorem. In the figure below, *AC* is the water's depth and the leg of right triangle *ABC*. The other leg, *BC*, is the distance from the reed to a side of the pool, given as 5 ft. When the reed is stretched to the side of the pool, it becomes the hypotenuse of the right triangle.

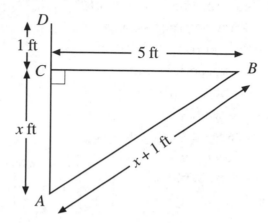

If we define the depth of the water *AC* as *x*, then *AD* = *x* + 1 is the length of the reed. Applying the Pythagorean theorem, we have

$$(x + 1)^2 = 5^2 + x^2$$

$$x^2 + 2x + 1 = 25 + x^2$$

$$2x = 24$$

$$x = 12 \text{ ft, the depth of the water}$$

$$x + 1 = 13 \text{ ft, the length of the reed}$$

Exalted Treasure of Jade

There is a treasure of jade buried in a wall. The exalted treasure is in the form of a right circular cylinder of unknown dimensions. When the wall is chiseled so that 1/10 ft of the depth of the jade is exposed, it can be seen that the axis of the cylinder is parallel to the face of the wall. The exposed part of the cross section of the cylinder is a segment of a circle whose chord measures 1 ft. What is the diameter of the jade cylinder?

Hint

In the sketch at the right, the chord of the circular cross section is segment *AB*.

Note

Problems of this type were solved as early as 200 B.C. during the Han dynasty in ancient China.

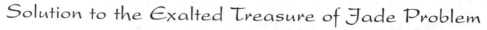

Solution to the Exalted Treasure of Jade Problem

The solution of the problem uses the basic properties of a circle and the Pythagorean theorem. The cross section of the jade cylinder is shown in Figure 1, where the parts of the problem are defined.

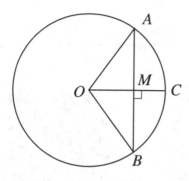

FIGURE 1

Given: Circle O with radius r

$$MC = \frac{1}{10} \text{ ft or } 0.1 \text{ ft}$$

$AB = 1$ ft

$AB \perp OC$ at M

$OA = OC = OB = r$

Find: d, the diameter of circle O

In Figure 2, we apply the Pythagorean theorem to right triangle OAM, using r as the common variable.

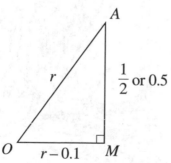

FIGURE 2

$$r^2 = (0.5)^2 + (r - 0.1)^2$$

$$r^2 = 0.25 + r^2 - 0.2r + 0.01$$

$$0.2r = 0.26$$

$$r = 1.3$$

$$\therefore d = 2r = 2.6 \text{ ft}$$

Precious Golden Rope

There is a precious rope of gold hanging from the bough of a willow tree. A learned philosopher sitting beneath the tree muses over the situation. He observes that when the rope hangs freely, 3 ft of rope is left over, after it makes contact with the ground. However, if the philosopher stretches the rope so that its free end just touches the ground, the free end is positioned 8 ft from where the rope first touched the ground. How long is the rope?

Solution to the Precious Golden Rope Problem

The figure on the left illustrates the rope at the time of first observation by the philosopher. Let x be the distance from the tree limb to the first contact point on the ground.

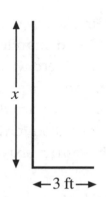

first contact position

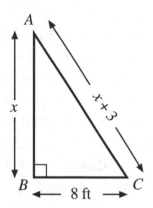

stretched position

The stretched position of the rope is shown in the figure on the right. The leg AB of the right triangle ABC is x, determined by the first contact position. Leg BC is 8 ft, the distance from the first contact position to the end of the rope in the stretched position. The hypotenuse AC is the length of the entire rope, or $x + 3$. If we apply the Pythagorean theorem to the right triangle ABC, it follows that

$$(x + 3)^2 = 8^2 + x^2$$

$$x^2 + 6x + 9 = 64 + x^2$$

$$6x = 55$$

$$x = 9\frac{1}{6} \text{ ft}$$

$$x + 3 = 12\frac{1}{6} \text{ ft, the length of the rope}$$

The Party's Over

The following problem from ancient China is found in the Han dynasty classic, the *Nine Chapters of Mathematical Art*.

The Problem

A bureaucrat going about his business of overseeing water use spotted a woman washing dishes in the river. Immediately, he demanded of her: "Why are there so many dishes here?" She replied, "There was a dinner party in the house." His next question was "How many guests attended the party?" She did not know but gave this reply: "Every two guests shared one dish for rice; every three guests used one dish for broth; every four guests used one dish for meat; and altogether, sixty-five dishes were used at the party."

If you had been at the river, could you have answered the questions of the overseer? How many guests attended the party?

Solution to The Party's Over Problem

The solution of this problem is based on fractional parts or ratio. From the information in the problem, we construct the following ratios and convert them to a form in which they share a lowest common denominator.

Rice: number of plates/guest $= \dfrac{1}{2} = \dfrac{6}{12}$

Broth: number of plates/guest $= \dfrac{1}{3} = \dfrac{4}{12}$

Meat: number of plates/guest $= \dfrac{1}{4} = \dfrac{3}{12}$

(Lowest common denominator, or LCD = 12)

By adding the three fractions (expressed with the LCD), we find the number of plates for rice, broth, and meat used by 12 guests.

$$\frac{6}{12} + \frac{4}{12} + \frac{3}{12} = \frac{13}{12} \text{ plates/guest}$$

Thus, it takes 13 plates to serve a complete meal for 12 guests. Interpret the fraction $\dfrac{13}{12}$ as a rate, r, or $r = \dfrac{13}{12}$ plates/guest.

As a rate problem, the following simple equation can be written:

$A = rn$,   where A = number of plates for all guests

r = number of plates/guest

n = number of guests

Therefore, $n = \dfrac{A}{r} = \dfrac{65 \text{ plates}}{13/12 \text{ plates/guests}} = 60$ guests

Answers and Solutions

Page 7, Exercise 1

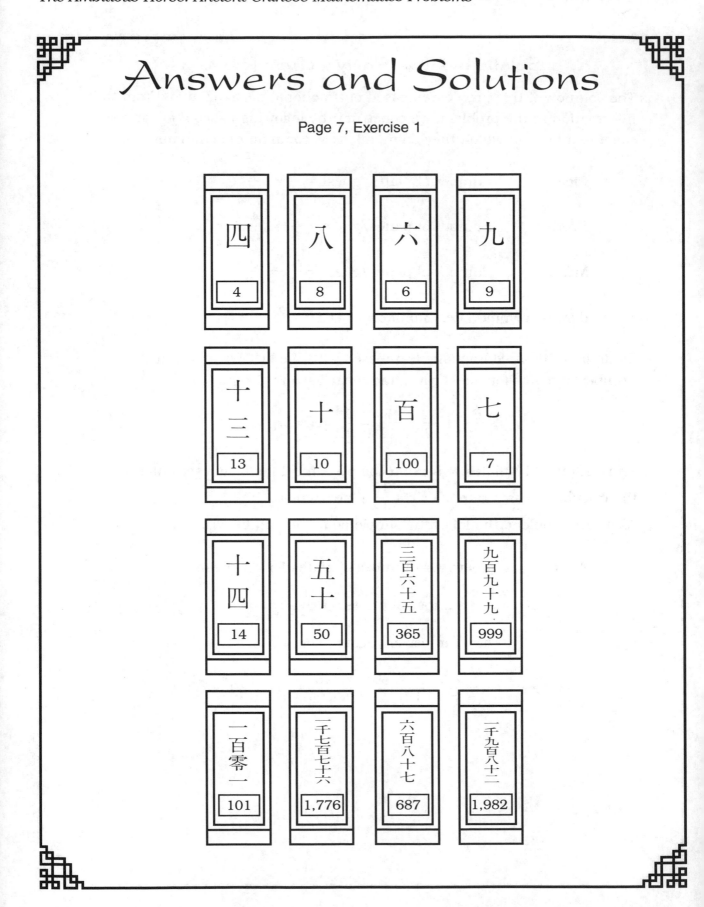

Page 8, Exercise 2

Pages 9–10, Exercise 3

a.

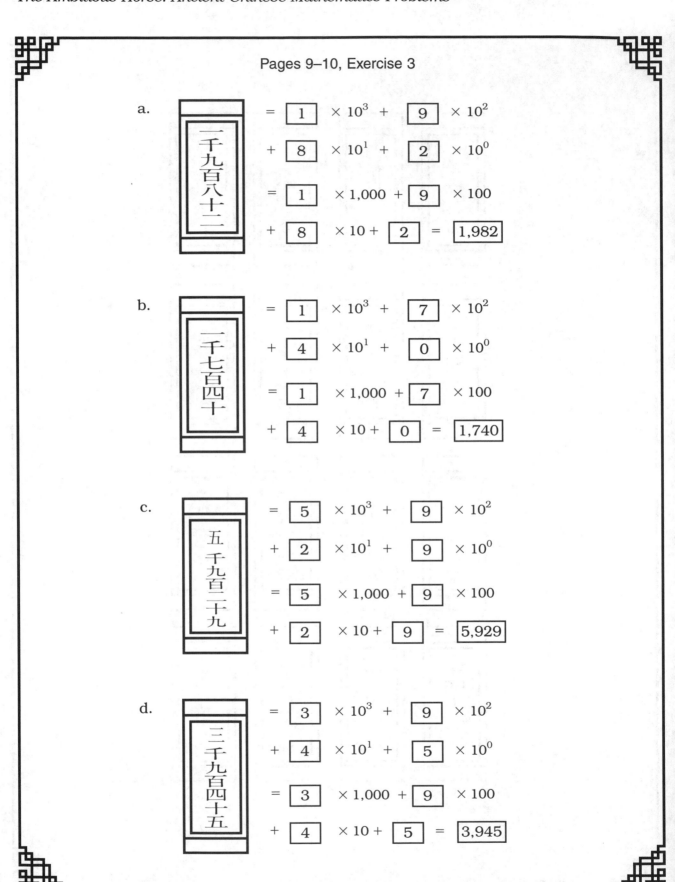

一千九百八十二

$= \boxed{1} \times 10^3 + \boxed{9} \times 10^2$

$+ \boxed{8} \times 10^1 + \boxed{2} \times 10^0$

$= \boxed{1} \times 1{,}000 + \boxed{9} \times 100$

$+ \boxed{8} \times 10 + \boxed{2} = \boxed{1{,}982}$

b.

一千七百四十

$= \boxed{1} \times 10^3 + \boxed{7} \times 10^2$

$+ \boxed{4} \times 10^1 + \boxed{0} \times 10^0$

$= \boxed{1} \times 1{,}000 + \boxed{7} \times 100$

$+ \boxed{4} \times 10 + \boxed{0} = \boxed{1{,}740}$

c.

五千九百二十九

$= \boxed{5} \times 10^3 + \boxed{9} \times 10^2$

$+ \boxed{2} \times 10^1 + \boxed{9} \times 10^0$

$= \boxed{5} \times 1{,}000 + \boxed{9} \times 100$

$+ \boxed{2} \times 10 + \boxed{9} = \boxed{5{,}929}$

d.

三千九百四十五

$= \boxed{3} \times 10^3 + \boxed{9} \times 10^2$

$+ \boxed{4} \times 10^1 + \boxed{5} \times 10^0$

$= \boxed{3} \times 1{,}000 + \boxed{9} \times 100$

$+ \boxed{4} \times 10 + \boxed{5} = \boxed{3{,}945}$

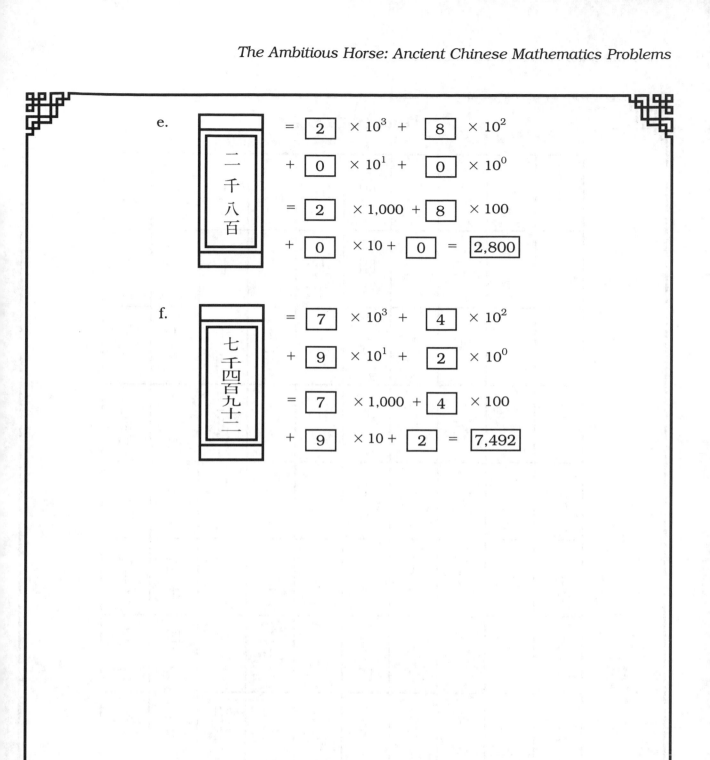

e.
二千八百

$= \boxed{2} \times 10^3 + \boxed{8} \times 10^2$

$+ \boxed{0} \times 10^1 + \boxed{0} \times 10^0$

$= \boxed{2} \times 1{,}000 + \boxed{8} \times 100$

$+ \boxed{0} \times 10 + \boxed{0} = \boxed{2{,}800}$

f.
七千四百九十二

$= \boxed{7} \times 10^3 + \boxed{4} \times 10^2$

$+ \boxed{9} \times 10^1 + \boxed{2} \times 10^0$

$= \boxed{7} \times 1{,}000 + \boxed{4} \times 100$

$+ \boxed{9} \times 10 + \boxed{2} = \boxed{7{,}492}$

Page 11, Exercise 4

	一	二	三	四	五	六	七	八	九
一	一	二	三	四	五	六	七	八	九
二	二	四	六	八	十	十二	十四	十六	十八
三	三	六	九	十二	十五	十八	二十一	二十四	二十七
四	四	八	十二	十六	二十	二十四	二十八	三十二	三十六
五	五	十	十五	二十	二十五	三十	三十五	四十	四十五
六	六	十二	十八	二十四	三十	三十六	四十二	四十八	五十四
七	七	十四	二十一	二十八	三十五	四十二	四十九	五十六	六十三
八	八	十六	二十四	三十二	四十	四十八	五十六	六十四	七十二
九	九	十八	二十七	三十六	四十五	五十四	六十三	七十二	八十一

Page 20, Exercise 1

Figure 5: 80,868 − 4,735 = 76,133

Figure 6: 7,998 − 5,273 = 2,725

Page 21, Exercise 2

a. 13,677   b. 97,895   c. 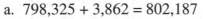   d.

e. 3,076   f.   g. h. 96,652

i.   j. 7,083,990

Page 22, Exercise 3

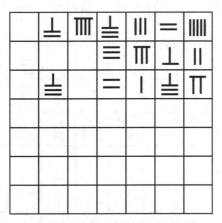

a. 798,325 + 3,862 = 802,187

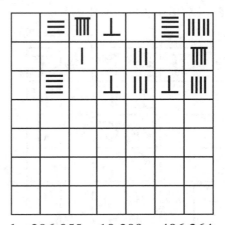

b. 396,055 + 10,309 = 406,364

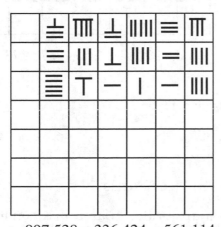

c. 897,538 − 336,424 = 561,114

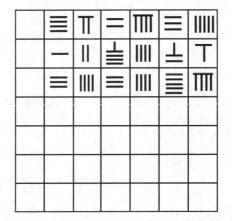

d. 472,935 − 129,476 = 343,459

Page 23, Exercise 4

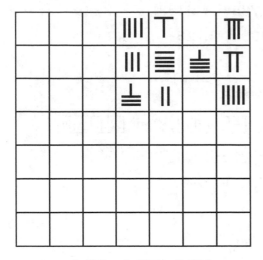

a. 4,608 + 3,597 = 8,205

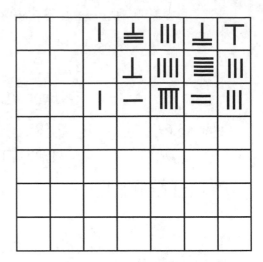

b. 18,376 – 6,453 = 11,923

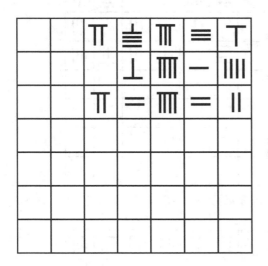

c. 79,836 – 6,914 = 72,922

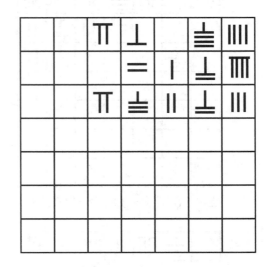

d. 76,094 + 2,179 = 78,273

Page 29, Exercise 1

a. 37 × 87   b. 465 × 867   c. 308 × 932

Page 31, Exercises: Seven-Piece Puzzle

2. 8 square units; 3. 8 square units; 8 square units; 4. area is a constant (8 units with given dimensions), independent of the shape.

Page 32, Exercise with the Dog

You could define a single closed region as a closed region in which you can connect any two points with a path that only contains points belonging to the closed region.

2. 8 square units

3.–7. Answers vary with the figures chosen in construction.

8. The square; $4 \cdot \sqrt{8} = 8\sqrt{2}$ units

9. An arrangement where the pieces pairwise only shared one point; $10(2 + \sqrt{2})$ units

Page 33, Chinese Dissections

As shown in the diagram at the left of the problem, dissect the parallelogram into a trapezoid and a triangle. In the diagram below, these dissections are trapezoid $ABFD$ and triangle BCF.

$FB \perp CD$ and $EA \perp CD$, because FB is the altitude and EA is constructed that way.

$FB = EA$, because both are the distances between the same parallel lines.

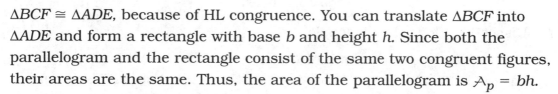

$AD = BC$, because $ABCD$ is a parallelogram.

$\triangle BCF \cong \triangle ADE$, because of HL congruence. You can translate $\triangle BCF$ into $\triangle ADE$ and form a rectangle with base b and height h. Since both the parallelogram and the rectangle consist of the same two congruent figures, their areas are the same. Thus, the area of the parallelogram is $A_p = bh$.

Dissect the parallelogram into two triangles as shown in the diagram below. $\triangle ABC \cong \triangle ADC$, because of SSS congruence. Thus, their areas are equal—and therefore $A_t = \frac{1}{2}bh$.

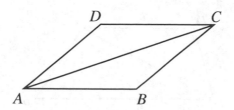

Page 34, Classic Theorem

Explanations can vary, but the following is one possible solution:

Draw altitude *CL* of Δ*ABC* from vertex *C*. Label the intersection of *CL* and *MN*, point *K*, as shown in the diagram.

L is also *C*'s mirror image over *MN*, because Δ*ACL* ~ Δ*MCK* (*MN* ∥ *AB* and *M* is a midpoint of *AC*).

Thus, *ML* = *MC* = *AM*, due to the property of reflection and because *M* is the midpoint of *AC*. So, Δ*AML* is isosceles. For similar reasons, *LN* = *CN* = *NB*, so Δ*LNB* is isosceles. *MX* and *NY* are perpendicular to *AB*, so they are the axes of symmetry for the isosceles triangles Δ*AML* and Δ*LNB*. Therefore, *L* is the mirror image of *A* over *MX* and of *B* over *NY*.

Because of the property of reflection as a transformation that preserves angle measures, ∠1 = ∠*A*, ∠2 = ∠*B*, and ∠3 = ∠*C*. Applying the angle addition postulate and substitution, we find that ∠1 + ∠2 + ∠3 = 180°, so ∠*A* + ∠*B* + ∠*C* = 180°.

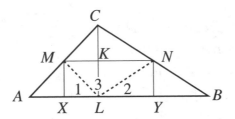

Page 35, Problem 1

A. Dissecting along the diagonal:

Refer to the diagram below. $A(ABCD) = A(\triangle ABC) + A(\triangle ACD)$. Δ*ABC*'s base is b_1 and its height is *h*, so $A(\triangle ABC) = \frac{1}{2}b_1 h$. For Δ*ACD*, we can choose b_2 (the trapezoid's second base) as its base. The height of the triangle will also be *h*, because the distance of vertex *A* from *DC* is the same as the distance between *C* and *AB*. $A(\triangle ACD) = \frac{1}{2}b_2 h$ and therefore, $A(ABCD) = \frac{1}{2}b_1 h + \frac{1}{2}b_2 h = \frac{1}{2}(b_1 + b_2)h$.

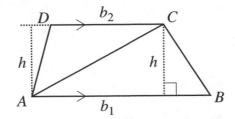

B. Dissecting through its bases:

Refer to the diagram below. Dissect the trapezoid into a parallelogram and a triangle. So, $A(ABCD) = A(ADCE) + A(ECB)$. $A(ADCE) = b_2 h$ and $A(ECB) = \frac{1}{2}(b_1 - b_2)h$. Thus, $A(ABCD) = b_2 h + \frac{1}{2}(b_1 - b_2)h = \frac{1}{2}(b_1 + b_2)h$.

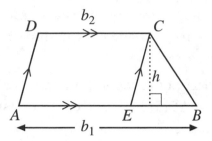

C. Dissecting along the median:

Refer to the diagram below. Draw in the perpendicular line segments through the endpoints of the median labeled E and F. $\triangle AGE \cong \triangle DJE$, because $AE = DE$ (EF is a median) and $\angle AEG = \angle DEJ$ (vertical angles). Both triangles have a right angle at G and J respectively, because JG was constructed that way. Thus, $A(AGE) = A(DJE)$. The same can be said of $\triangle HBF$ and $\triangle ICF$, therefore $A(HBF) = A(ICF)$. So, $A(ABCD) = A(GHIJ)$.

And $A(GHIJ) = EF \cdot h$, and because $EF = JI = GH$,

$2 \cdot EF = b_1 - x - y + b_2 + x + y = b_1 + b_2$,

so $EF = \frac{1}{2}(b_1 + b_2)$ and $A(GHIJ) = EF \cdot h = \frac{1}{2}(b_1 + b_2)h$

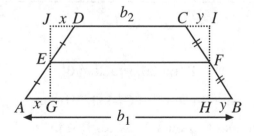

Page 35, Problem 2

Interior angles of an obtuse triangle:

Either draw in the midsegment just as you did on page 34, connecting the two shorter sides (turn the triangle on its longest side as base), or draw in the midsegment as shown on the diagram below. *CD* is the altitude from vertex *C*. *EF* ∥ *AB*, so *CD* ⊥ *EF*. Because △*CDA* ~ △*CGE*, and *E* is a midpoint, *CG* = *GD*. Therefore, *C*'s mirror image over midline *EF* is *D*. Thus, △*CEF* ≅ △*DEF* and ∠*ECF* = ∠*EDF*.

CF = *DF* due to the property of reflection and *CF* = *FB* because *F* is a midpoint, so *DF* = *FB* and △*DFB* is isosceles. Because the base angles of an isosceles triangle are equal, ∠*FBD* = ∠*FDB*.

By the same reasoning, *CE* = *DE* because of reflection and *CE* = *EA* because *E* is a midpoint, so *DE* = *EA* and △*DEA* is isosceles. Since the base angles of an isosceles triangle are equal, ∠*EDA* = ∠*EAD*.

∠*CAD* = 180° − ∠*CAB*, because they are supplementary.

From the last two steps, knowing that ∠*EDA* = ∠*EAD*, we find that ∠*EDF* + ∠*FDA* = 180° − ∠*CAB*, therefore ∠*EDF* + ∠*FDA* + ∠*CAB* = 180°. And because ∠*EDF* = ∠*ACB* and ∠*FDA* = ∠*B*, we get ∠*ACB* + ∠*B* + ∠*CAB* = 180°.

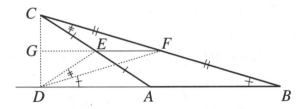

Page 35, Problem 3

Refer to the figure on page 34 for the Classic Theorem problem.

Label the common vertex of angles 1, 2, and 3, point *L*.

△*AMX* ≅ △*LMX*, △*CMN* ≅ △*LMN*, and △*BYN* ≅ △*LYN*, therefore:
$\mathcal{A}(XYNM) = \frac{1}{2}\mathcal{A}(ABC)$. $\mathcal{A}(XYNM) = XY \cdot YN$. $YN = \frac{1}{2}h$ and $XY = \frac{1}{2}AB$, so $\mathcal{A}(ABC) = 2 \cdot \frac{1}{2}h \cdot \frac{1}{2}AB = \frac{1}{2}AB \cdot h$.

Page 35, Problem 4

Refer to the diagram below.

The diagonals of a rhombus are perpendicular bisectors of each other, so they intersect to form four congruent right triangles with legs $\frac{1}{2}d_1$ and $\frac{1}{2}d_2$. Therefore, the area of the rhombus is

$$4(\frac{1}{2})(\frac{1}{2}d_1)(\frac{1}{2}d_2) = \frac{1}{2}d_1d_2$$

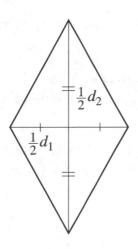

Page 35, Problem 5

Refer to the diagram below.

By definition, regular polygons have equal sides (s). Connecting the center of the circumscribed circle to the vertices, we divide the pentagon into five congruent triangles (SSS). Thus, the apothems (a) are equal.

$\mathcal{A}(\text{pentagon}) = 5\mathcal{A}(\text{triangle}) = 5 \cdot \frac{1}{2} \cdot \text{side} \cdot \text{apothem}$
$= \frac{1}{2} \cdot (5 \text{ side}) \cdot \text{apothem} = \frac{1}{2} \cdot \text{perimeter} \cdot \text{apothem}.$

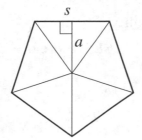

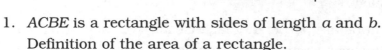

Page 37, Liu Hui's Solution
Reasons for Steps

1. *ACBE* is a rectangle with sides of length *a* and *b*.
   Definition of the area of a rectangle.

2. *CDFG* and *ACBE* are both comprised of two regions identical to region 1 (small triangles), two regions identical to region 2 (large triangles), and two regions identical to region 3 (square). So, their areas are equal.

3. Definition of rectangle area, and by construction.

4. Substitution.

5. Division property of equality. $(a + b) \neq 0$, because $a > 0$ and $b > 0$ being measures of the sides of a triangle.

Page 38, Western Solution
Reasons for Steps

1. Area addition postulate.

2. Area formula for a triangle.
   Distributive law.

3. Area formula for a triangle.
   Distributive law.

4. Area formula for a square.

5. Area formula for a triangle.

6. Substitution of (2), (3), (4), and (5) into (1).

7. Multiplication property of equality.

8. Addition of like terms.

9. Distributive law.

10. Division property of equality.

An alternate solution: $\triangle BAC \sim \triangle BEF$, therefore $EF/AC = BF/BC$ and $\frac{s}{b} = \frac{a - s}{a}$ so $s = \frac{ab}{a + b}$

Page 40, More from Liu Hui

The radii shown in Figure 1 are perpendicular to sides. *AO* and *CO* are the hypotenuses of congruent right triangles (marked as 1's and 2's), because of *HL* congruency.

Obviously one can create rectangle *EFGH* by pairing right triangles as shown in the diagram.

The following are reasons for each step.

1. *ABCD* is a rectangle with sides of length *a* and *b*.
   Area postulate for rectangle.

2. *EFGH* consists of double the parts as *ABCD*. Therefore, the area of *EFGH* is twice that of *ABCD*.

3. Area postulate for rectangle.

4. Substitution.

5. Division property of equality.

Page 41, Western Solution
Reasons for Steps

1. Area addition postulate.

2. Area formulas for a triangle and a square.

3. Segment addition property.

4. Substitution of (3) into (2).

5. Multiplication property of equality.

6. Addition of like terms.

7. Distributive law.

8. Division property of equality.

9. Definition of diameter.

10. Multiplication property of equality and substitution.

Page 45, Proof
Reasons for Steps

1. Definitions given in problem.

2. Since $\triangle APE \sim \triangle ESG$, $AP/PE = ES/SG$, or $(AP)(SG) = (ES)(PE)$. $AP = QE$ and $EK = SG$, because of construction, so by substitution we get $\mathcal{A}(QUKE) = \mathcal{A}(PESC)$. These areas are complementary with respect to diagonal AG. $\mathcal{A}(QUKE) = \mathcal{A}(LWJF)$, because of construction ($SG = TI$).

3. Complementary areas with respect to diagonal AB.

4. Subtraction property of equality.

5. Area addition property.
   Substitution.

6. Definition for the area of a rectangle.

7. Substitution.

8. Segment addition property (since $TI = SG = s_1$ by construction).

9. Substitution.
   Definitions in problem.

10. Division property of equality.

11. Segment addition property.
    Definitions in problem.
    Substitution.

Page 48, Proof
Reasons for Steps

1. Definitions given in problem.

2. Since $\triangle APE \sim \triangle ESG$, $AP/PE = ES/SG$, or $(AP)(SG) = (ES)(PE)$. $AP = QE$ and $EK = SG$, because of construction, so by substitution we get $\mathcal{A}(QUKE) = \mathcal{A}(PESC)$. These areas are complementary with respect to diagonal AH. $\mathcal{A}(QUKE) = \mathcal{A}(LWJF)$, because of construction ($SG = TI$).

3. Complementary areas with respect to diagonal AB.

4. Subtraction property of equality.

5. Area addition property.
   Substitution.

6. Definition for the area of a rectangle.
   Definitions in problem.

7. Substitution.

8. Segment addition property.
   Definitions in problem.

9. Substitution.

10. Division property of equality.

11. Segment addition property.
    Definitions in problem.
    Substitution.

12. Area formula applied in step 2.

13. Definitions in problem.

14. Substitution from lines 10, 12, and 13.
    Division property of equality.

Page 50, Yin-Yang Proof
Answers for Given and Prove

Given: Circle *O* with diameter *AB*; semicircles *AXO* and
OYB with diameters equal to $\dfrac{AB}{2}$

Prove: $\mathcal{A}(S) = \mathcal{A}(R)$; $\mathsf{L}(AXOYB) = \dfrac{1}{2}$(circumference)

Reasons for Steps

1. Given.

2. Area addition postulate.

3. Congruent semicircles have equal areas.

4. Substitution.

5. Substitution.

6. Arc addition postulate.

7. Circumference formula.

8. Substitution.

9. Distributive law of multiplication over addition.

10. Circumference formula.

Page 51, More Yin-Yang!
Part 1

Algebraic Proof for $\mathcal{A}(R) = \mathcal{A}(S) = \mathcal{A}(T)$

1. $AB = BC = CD$

2. Areas of semicircles:

$$\mathcal{A}_1 = \mathcal{A}(AXB) = \frac{1}{2}\pi\left(\frac{AB}{2}\right)^2 = \frac{\pi}{8}(AB)^2$$

$$\mathcal{A}_2 = \mathcal{A}(CID) = \frac{1}{2}\pi\left(\frac{CD}{2}\right)^2 = \frac{\pi}{8}(CD)^2 = \frac{\pi}{8}(AB)^2$$

$$\mathcal{A}_3 = \mathcal{A}(AYC) = \frac{1}{2}\pi\left(\frac{AC}{2}\right)^2 = \frac{\pi}{2}(AB)^2$$

$$\mathcal{A}_4 = \mathcal{A}(BHD) = \frac{1}{2}\pi\left(\frac{BD}{2}\right)^2 = \frac{\pi}{2}(AB)^2$$

$$\mathcal{A}_5 = \mathcal{A}(ALD) = \frac{1}{2}\pi\left(\frac{3AB}{2}\right)^2 = \frac{9\pi}{8}(AB)^2$$

$$\mathcal{A}_6 = \mathcal{A}(AMD) = \mathcal{A}(ALD) = \frac{9\pi}{8}(AB)^2$$

3. $\mathcal{A}(R) = \mathcal{A}_1 + \mathcal{A}_6 - \mathcal{A}_4 = \frac{\pi}{8}(AB)^2 + \frac{9\pi}{8}(AB)^2 - \frac{\pi}{2}(AB)^2$

$$= \frac{3\pi}{4}(AB)^2 = \frac{1}{3}\left[\frac{9\pi}{4}(AB)^2\right] = \frac{1}{3}(\text{area of circle } O)$$

4. $\mathcal{A}(S) = \mathcal{A}_3 - \mathcal{A}_1 + \mathcal{A}_4 - \mathcal{A}_2$

$$= \frac{\pi}{2}(AB)^2 - \frac{\pi}{8}(AB)^2 + \frac{\pi}{2}(AB)^2 - \frac{\pi}{8}(AB)^2 = \frac{3\pi}{4}(AB)^2$$

5. $\mathcal{A}(T) = \mathcal{A}_2 + \mathcal{A}_5 - \mathcal{A}_3 = \frac{\pi}{8}(AB)^2 + \frac{9\pi}{8}(AB)^2 - \frac{\pi}{2}(AB)^2$

$$= \frac{3\pi}{4}(AB)^2$$

From lines 3, 4, and 5, it follows by substitution that

6. $\mathcal{A}(R) = \mathcal{A}(S) = \mathcal{A}(T)$

$\mathcal{Q.E.D.}$

Page 51, More Yin-Yang!

Part 2

Algebraic Proof for ∟(*AXBHD*) = ∟(*AYCID*)

1. ∟(*AXBHD*) = ∟(*AXB*) + ∟(*BHD*)

   ∟(*AYCID*) = ∟(*AYC*) + ∟(*CID*)

2. ∟(*AXB*) = $\pi\dfrac{AB}{2}$

   ∟(*CID*) = $\pi\dfrac{AB}{2}$

   ∟(*BHD*) = $\pi\dfrac{BD}{2} = \pi(AB)$

   ∟(*AYC*) = $\pi\dfrac{AC}{2} = \pi(AB)$

3. ∟(*AXBHD*) = $\dfrac{\pi}{2}(AB) + \pi(AB) = \dfrac{3\pi}{2}(AB)$

   ∟(*AYCID*) = $\pi(AB) + \dfrac{\pi}{2}(AB) = \dfrac{3\pi}{2}(AB)$

4. ∟(*AXBHD*) = ∟(*AYCID*) = $\dfrac{\pi}{2}(3AB) = \dfrac{\pi}{2}(AD)$

   $= \dfrac{1}{2}[\pi(AD)]$

   $= \dfrac{1}{2}$[circumference of circle *O*]

   Q.E.D.

Page 52, Another Case of Yin-Yang!

Part 1

Algebraic Proof for $A(R) = A(S) = A(T) = A(U)$

1. $AB = BO = OC = CD$

2.   Areas of semicircles:

$$A_1 = A(AXB) = \frac{\pi}{8}(AB)^2; \qquad A_2 = A(CJD) = \frac{\pi}{8}(AB)^2;$$

$$A_3 = A(AYO) = \frac{\pi}{2}(AB)^2; \qquad A_4 = A(OID) = \frac{\pi}{2}(AB)^2;$$

$$A_5 = A(AZC) = \frac{9\pi}{8}(AB)^2; \qquad A_6 = A(BHD) = \frac{9\pi}{8}(AB)^2;$$

$$A_7 = A(ALD) = 2\pi(AB)^2; \qquad A_8 = A(AMD) = 2\pi(AB)^2$$

3. $A(R) = A_1 + A_8 - A_6 = \frac{\pi}{8}(AB)^2 + 2\pi(AB)^2 - \frac{9\pi}{8}(AB)^2 = \pi(AB)^2$

4. $A(S) = A_3 - A_1 + A_6 - A_4$

$$= \frac{\pi}{2}(AB)^2 - \frac{\pi}{8}(AB)^2 + \frac{9\pi}{8}(AB)^2 - \frac{\pi}{2}(AB)^2$$

$$= \pi(AB)^2$$

5. $A(T) = A_5 - A_3 + A_4 - A_2$

$$= \frac{9\pi}{8}(AB)^2 - \frac{\pi}{2}(AB)^2 + \frac{\pi}{2}(AB)^2 - \frac{\pi}{8}(AB)^2$$

$$= \pi(AB)^2$$

6. $A(U) = A_7 - A_5 + A_2 = 2\pi(AB)^2 - \frac{9\pi}{8}(AB)^2 + \frac{\pi}{8}(AB)^2 = \pi(AB)^2$

7.   From lines 3, 4, 5, and 6, it follows by substitution that

$A(R) = A(S) = A(T) = A(U)$

Q.E.D.

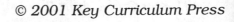

Page 52, Another Case of Yin-Yang!
Part 2

Algebraic Proof for ∟(*AXBHD*) = ∟(*AYOID*) = ∟(*AZCJD*)

1. ∟(*AXBHD*) = ∟(*AXB*) + ∟(*BHD*)

    ∟(*AYOID*) = ∟(*AYO*) + ∟(*OID*)

    ∟(*AZCJD*) = ∟(*AZC*) + ∟(*CJD*)

2. $\angle(AXB) = \frac{\pi}{2}(AB)$; $\angle(CJD) = \frac{\pi}{2}(AB)$

    $\angle(BHD) = \frac{3\pi}{2}(AB)$; $\angle(AZC) = \frac{3\pi}{2}(AB)$

    ∟(*AYO*) = π(*AB*); ∟(*OID*) = π(*AB*)

3. $\angle(AXBHD) = \frac{\pi}{2}(AB) + \frac{3\pi}{2}(AB) = 2\pi(AB)$

4. ∟(*AYOID*) = π(*AB*) + π(*AB*) = 2π(*AB*)

5. $\angle(AZCJD) = \frac{3\pi}{2}(AB) + \frac{\pi}{2}(AB) = 2\pi(AB)$

6. From lines 3, 4, and 5, it follows that

    ∟(*AXBHD*) = ∟(*AYOID*) = ∟(*AZCJD*) = 2π(*AB*)

    $= \frac{1}{2}[\pi(AD)]$

    $= \frac{1}{2}[\text{circumference of circle } O]$

    Q.E.D.

Page 53, General Yin-Yang!

Algebraic Proof for $\llcorner(AXPYD) = \frac{1}{2}\pi(AD)$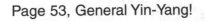

1. $\llcorner(AXP) = \frac{1}{2}\pi(AP)$

   $\llcorner(DYP) = \frac{1}{2}\pi(PD)$

2. $\llcorner(AXPYD) = \llcorner(AXP) + \llcorner(DYP)$

3. $\llcorner(AXPYD) = \frac{1}{2}\pi(AP) + \frac{1}{2}\pi(PD)$

4. $\llcorner(AXPYD) = \frac{1}{2}\pi(AP + PD)$

5. But $AD = AP + PD$

   $\llcorner(AXPYD) = \frac{1}{2}\pi(AD)$ Q.E.D.

Note: $\llcorner(AXPYD) = \frac{1}{2}\pi(AD) = \frac{1}{2}$[circumference of circle O]

or, in other words, the length of the path of the two semicircular arcs has a total length of one-half of the circumference of the circle, independent of the choice of P on the diameter AD.

Page 56, Zhou Exercise

1. Answers can vary.

2. $\triangle AFB \cong \triangle BGC \cong \triangle CHD \cong \triangle DEA$, because of SAS congruence of triangles. Therefore, $AB = BC = CD = DA$. $\angle BAF = \angle CBG$, because of congruence of triangles. Similarly $\angle ABF = \angle BCG$. From right $\triangle AFB$ we have that $\angle BAF + \angle ABF = 90°$ and $\angle BAF = \angle CBG$, so $\angle ABF + \angle CBG = 90°$. $\angle ABF + \angle CBG + \angle ABC = 180°$, because they form a straight angle. Therefore, $\angle ABC = 90°$ and quadrilateral $ABCD$ is a square. The areas of the four congruent triangles $\triangle AKB$, $\triangle BKC$, $\triangle CID$, and $\triangle DJA$ are equal to 6 units each. So, the area of square $ABCD$ is 25 square units, therefore the length of its side is 5 units.

   And from the Pythagorean theorem: $3^2 + 4^2 = 5^2$

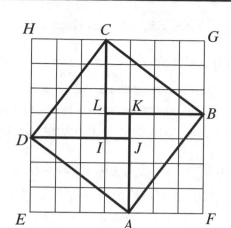

3. A square with side 3 cannot be inscribed in a square with side 5.

   Yes, the difference is a perfect square. $25 - 9 = 16$, $5^2 - 3^2 = 4^2$ or $3^2 + 4^2 = 5^2$.

4. The difference in area of the square with side 5 and the inscribed square of side 4 is 9, a perfect square. Hence, $25 - 16 = 9$, $5^2 - 4^2 = 3^2$ or $3^2 + 4^2 = 5^2$ satisfies the property of the Pythagorean theorem.

5. Let x be the length of one leg of a right triangle, then $5 - x$ is the length of the other leg. The hypotenuse is equal to 4.

   Applying the Pythagorean theorem, we have

   $x^2 + (5 - x)^2 = 16$

   $x^2 + 25 - 10x + x^2 = 16$

   $2x^2 - 10x + 9 = 0$

   By applying the quadratic formula, we have

   $x = \dfrac{5 \pm \sqrt{7}}{2}$

   Alternatively, the area of the triangle is $\dfrac{9}{4}$.

   $\dfrac{1}{2}(x)(5 - x) = \dfrac{9}{4}$

   $5x - x^2 = \dfrac{9}{2}$ or $2x^2 - 10x + 9 = 0$, which leads

   to the same result above: $x = \dfrac{5 \pm \sqrt{7}}{2}$.

Page 58, Gou-Gu Theorem

The congruence of triangles 2 and 5 is true for the following reasons:

AB = *CD*, because *ABCD* is a square. ∠*DKC* = ∠*AFB* = 90°, because *EGBF* is a square and *DK* is constructed to be perpendicular to *EC*. And ∠*KCD* = ∠*FBA*, because they are corresponding angles.

The congruence of triangles 1 and 4, and 3 and 6:

Because of the congruence of Δ*DKC* and Δ*AFB*, *DK* = *AF* and *EL* = *DK*, so *AF* = *EL* and therefore *EF* = *AL*. Also *GB* = *EF*, so *GB* = *AL*. *AD* = *BC*, because *ABCD* is a square, so Δ*ALD* ≅ Δ*BGC*. *IC* = *GC*, because *HGCI* is a square. From the congruence of Δ*AFB* and Δ*CGB*, *GC* = *AF*, and *AF* = *EL* = *DK*, so *GC* = *DK* and *CI* = *DK*. Thus Δ*BGC* and square *HGCI* can be translated by vector *CD* and the images will be Δ*ALD* and square *ELDK*.

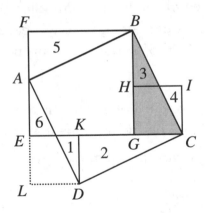

Page 99, The Party's Over

Alternate solution for the problem:

Let *n* be the number of guests.

So, $\dfrac{n}{2} + \dfrac{n}{3} + \dfrac{n}{4} = 65$

$6n + 4n + 3n = 780$

$13n = 780$

$n = 60$

Mathematics Bibliography

Boyer, Carl B. *A History of Mathematics.* New York: Wiley, 1968.

Cullen, Christopher. *Astronomy and Mathematics in Ancient China: The Zhou Bi Suan Jing.* Cambridge University Press, 1996.

Martzloff, Jean-Claude. *A History of Chinese Mathematics.* Heidelberg: Springer Verlag, 1997.

Menninger, Karl. *Number Words and Number Symbols: A Cultural History of Numbers.* New York: Dover Publications, 1948.

Mikami, Yoshio. *The Development of Mathematics in China and Japan.* 2nd ed. New York: Chelsea Publishing Co., 1974.

Needham, Joseph. *Science and Civilisation in China.* Vols 1–5. Cambridge University Press, 1959.

Neugebauer, Otto. *The Exact Sciences in Antiquity.* New York: Dover Publications, 1969.

Ore, Oystein. *Number Theory and Its History.* New York: Dover Publications, 1948.

Read, Ronald C. *Tangrams; 330 Puzzles.* New York: Dover Publications, 1965.

Smith, David E. *History of Mathematics.* New York: Dover Publications, 1951.

Swetz, Frank J. *The Sea Island Mathematical Manual: Surveying and Mathematics in Ancient China.* Pennsylvania State University Press, 1992.

Yan, Li, and Dù Shírán. *Chinese Mathematics: A Concise History.* Oxford: Clarendon Press, 1987.

Art Bibliography

Cahill, James. *Chinese Painting*. Geneva: Editions d'Art Albert Skira S.A., 1995.

Hawley, Willis M. *Chinese Folk Designs*. New York: Dover Publications, 1949.

Ho, Wai-Kam, editor, *The Century of Tung Ch'i-ch'ang 1555–1636*, Vols 1–2. Seattle: University of Washington Press, 1992.

Juliano, Annette L. *The Treasures of China*. New York: Richard Marek Publishers, 1981.

MacFarquhar, Roderick, et al. *The Forbidden City*. New York: Newsweek, 1978.

Paludan, Ann. *Chronicle of the Chinese Emperors*. London: Thames and Hudson, 1998.

Rawson, Jessica L., ed. *Mysteries of Ancient China: New Discoveries from the Early Dynasties*. New York: George Braziller, 1996.

Smith, Bradley, and Wan-go Weng. *China: A History in Art*. New York: Doubleday, 1979.

Pronunciation Guide

Vowels and Diphthongs		Consonants		
a	father	b		bike
e	her	p		pike
i	see	m		mother
u	hoof	f		five
ü	buick	d		dog
ai	bike	t		tea
ei	page	n		night, ink
ao	house	l		luck
ou	oath	g		give
an	land	k		kind
en	mention	h		house
in	tin	j		gin
ang	Hong Kong	q [ch]		
eng	length	x [hs]		
ing	thing	z [tz]		
ong	bassoon[g]	c [ts]		
er	far	s		see
ia	Maya	zh [dj]		george
ie	hear	ch		chicken
iu	you	sh		she
ian	Ian			
iang	young			
ua	quadruple			
ui	quick			
uan	twenty			
un	soon			

Note: The i after "z," "c," "s," "zh," "ch," and "sh" is pronounced like ə (schwa).

ba	ba	Rong Fang	rong-fang
Ba Gua	ba-gwa	san	san
bai	bai	Siyuan yujian xicao	si-yuan-yü-jian-hsi-tsao
Beijing	bei-jing	Shang	shang
Chen Zi	chen-tzi	Shang Gao	shang-gao
cheng	cheng	shang wei	shang-wei
Daxie shumu zi	da-hsie-shu-mu-tzi	shi	shi
er	ar	shou	shou
gou	gou	Shushu jiuzhang	shu-shu-jiu-djang
Gou-Gu	gou-gu	si	si
gu	gu	Song	song
Haidao suanjing	hai-dao-swan-jing	Sun	sun
Han	han	Sunzi suanjing	sun-tzi-swan-jing
Han Gaozu	han-gao-tzu	Tang	tang
Jia Xian	jia-hsian	wan	wan
Jing xi zi zhi	jing-hsi-tzi-dji	Wei	wei
jiu	jiu	wu	wu
Jiuzhang suanshu	jiu-djang-swan-shu	xia wei	hsia-wei
Kangxi	kang-hsi	xian	hsian
Kong Qiu	kong-chiu	Xiangjie jiuzhang suanfa	hsiang-jie-jiu-djang-swan-fa
kung-fu	kung-fu	Yang Hui	yang-hui
le	le	yi	yi
li	li	Yin-Yang	yin-yang
ling	ling	Yongzheng	yong-djeng
liu	liu	yu	yü
Liu Hui	liu-hui	Yuan	yüan
Manchu	man-chu	Zhang Qiujian	djang chiu-jian
Meng	meng	Zhang Qiujian suanjing	djang chiu-jian-swan-jing
Meng Tian	meng-tian	zhong wei	djong-wei
Ming	ming	Zhou	djou
qi	chi	Zhoubi	djou-bi
qian	chian	Zhoubi suanjing	djou-bi-swan-jing
Qin	chin	Zhu Shijie	dju-shi-jie
Qin Jiushao	chin-jiu-shao		
Qin Shihuangdi	chin-shi-hwang-di		
Qing	ching		